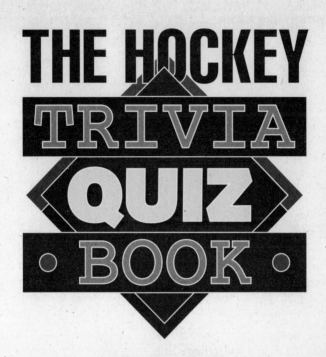

THE HOCKEY TRIVIA QUIZ BOOK

Don Weekes

GREYSTONE BOOKS
Douglas & McIntyre
Vancouver/Toronto

For Dorothy and Karen

Copyright © 1992 by Don Weekes
96 97 98 99 00   10 9 8 7 6

All rights reserved. No part of this book may be reproduced or transmitted in any form by any means without permission in writing from the publisher, except by a reviewer, who may quote brief passages in a review.

Greystone Books
A division of Douglas & McIntyre Ltd.
1615 Venables Street
Vancouver, British Columbia V5L 2H1

Canadian Cataloguing in Publication Data

Weekes, Don.
    The hockey trivia quiz book
ISBN 1-55054-061-0

1. Hockey — Miscellanea. 2. National Hockey League — Miscellanea.
I. Title.
GV847.W43 1992   796.962   C92-091717-8

Editing by Brian Scrivener
Design and typesetting by Robin Brass Studio
Jacket design by Eric Ansley & Associates Ltd.
Cover photo by Michael Digirolamo/Bruce Bennett Studios

Printed and bound in Canada by Best Book Manufacturers Inc.

Don Weekes still plays street hockey in Montreal, where he is a television writer and field producer for CFCF TV's sports magazine, "Hockey World."

CONTENTS

PREFACE

This book is for everyone who has ever wondered: Whatever happened to the four-on-four manpower situation? Who invented the slapshot? What NHL team won the Stanley Cup with the worst regular-season record? Where did Wayne Gretzky get the idea for No. 99?

From a fan's perspective, the quiz format is an ideal way to present a collection of hockey's greatest short stories and some of its more unusual statistical records. After all, hockey is a game, and outplaying the opposition is the goal. Here, the challenge is to figure out the right answer to questions on a wide range of hockey topics dating back to the first Stanley Cup a century ago.

Even if you weren't around to watch the electrifying Eddie Shore or witness the 1944 Cup finals featuring Rocket Richard or see the ground-breaking 1972 Canada–Soviet Summit Series, your chances of scoring points are good. The questions are of general interest (current to mid-1992). And the book is designed to be one great big quiz. The answer to one question sometimes provides a clue to the next multiple-choice or to the games and puzzles.

I gratefully acknowledge the cooperation of Phil Pritchard at the Hockey Hall of Fame, Danny Gallivan, Debra Schram, Ron Reusch of CFCF TV and Riel Lazarus, the most astute 16-year-old hockey fan in Montreal. I would also like to thank my editor, Pat Ryffranck, graphic artist Ivor Tiltin and crossword designer Adrian van Vlaardingen.

Ladies and gentlemen, sharpen your minds and your pencils. First period action is coming up!

DON WEEKES
July 1992

CHAPTER 1

THE PRE-GAME SKATE

Like hockey's pre-game skate (a custom dating back to the era of unheated rinks), this warm-up quiz offers something for everyone to get the adrenalin flowing. Sharpen your blades, tape your stick and try blowing a slapshot past these opening questions. Are you ready for the big leagues?

(Answers are at the end of the chapter.)

1.1 The NHL's official puck supplier is:

A. General Tire
B. Inglas Co.
C. Converse Rubber
D. Goodyear

1.2 After Maurice Richard, who was the second player to score 50 goals in 50 games?

A. Mike Bossy
B. Wayne Gretzky
C. Phil Esposito
D. Bobby Hull

1.3 What was the No. 1 hockey rule Walter Gretzky taught his son Wayne?

A. Practise, practise, practise.
B. Go where the puck's going, not where it's been.
C. Don't get "bigheaded."
D. When taking a pass, never look back.

1.4 How much did Gordie Howe receive as his 1991 NHL pension?

A. $13,000
B. $26,000
C. $52,000
D. $104,000

1.5 What NHL policy is a result of Eric Lindros not signing with the Quebec Nordiques?

A. No player can refuse to sign once drafted.
B. Clubs can negotiate prior to the draft.
C. Any drafted player refusing to sign loses NHL eligibility for two years.
D. Drafted players have limited freedom of club choice.

1.6 Which NHL building is graced by a picture of Queen Elizabeth above the ice?

A. Edmonton's Northlands Coliseum
B. Quebec Colisée
C. Winnipeg Arena
D. Vancouver's Pacific Coliseum

1.7 How much did ticket prices rise at St. Louis Arena after Brett Hull signed his four-year, $7.1-million contract with the Blues in 1990?

A. Prices stayed the same.
B. $3
C. $4
D. $5

1.8 **What children's song is unofficially banned by the NHL?**

A. "Humpty Dumpty"
B. "Three Blind Mice"
C. "Here We Go Round the Mulberry Bush"
D. "Rock-a-Bye Baby"

1.9 **Who said to Bobby Orr: "Kid, I don't know what the f*** they're paying you, but it's not enough"?**

A. Orr's agent, Alan Eagleson
B. Bruins veteran Ted Green
C. Teammate Phil Esposito
D. Bruins head scout Wren Blair

1.10 **Who was Lady Byng?**

A. The wife of NHL president Frank Calder
B. The wife of Canada's governor general
C. The NHL's first female executive
D. England's Duchess of York

1.11 **Who bellowed: "Let's get something straight — I wouldn't trade Ian Turnbull for God"?**

A. Maple Leafs owner Harold Ballard
B. Kings GM George Maguire
C. Colorado coach Don Cherry
D. Maple Leafs coach Roger Neilson

1.12 **What was Pat Burns's profession before he turned to NHL coaching?**

A. Sports psychologist
B. Country & western singer
C. Policeman
D. Charismatic healer

THE PRE-GAME SKATE
Answers

1.1 B. Inglas Co.

Since 1991, the Quebec-based Inglas Co. has been the sole supplier of NHL pucks, manufacturing about 5,000 game pucks and 10,000 practice pucks per team annually. Game pucks are injection-moulded and made of better-quality rubber than practice pucks, which are compressed into the standard disk shape. How to tell them apart? They're identical except for a tiny injection mark on the game puck's rim.

1.2 A. Mike Bossy.

Both Hull and Esposito came within a couple of games of 50-in-50, but it took Bossy to do it again — 36 years after Richard's 1944–45 feat and just one year before Gretzky set the all-time record of 50-in-39 during his dazzling 1981–82 season.

1.3 B. Go where the puck's going, not where it's been.

Wayne's first and most important coach was his dad. The elder Gretzky taught his son about practising, avoiding over-confidence and keeping his head up, but his No. 1 rule was: know where the play is heading and be there.

1.4 A. $13,000.

After 26 years in the NHL, hockey's greatest athlete and ambassador received a pension of $13,000 a year.

1.5 B. Clubs can negotiate prior to the draft.

Any club drafting first overall is allowed to bargain and sign a player before the NHL draft. Once the first pick has been signed, the team choosing second can begin negotiations with the second pick overall.

1.6 C. Winnipeg Arena.

For as long as anyone can remember, a portrait of Queen Elizabeth has hung in the arena. The current portrait was painted in 1979 to commemorate the arena's expansion to 15,393 seats. It's actually the second painting of the Queen commissioned to mark that occasion; the first was taken down when patrons noticed that it bore a striking resemblance to Marg Osborne, the Canadian singer best known for her appearances on "Don Messer's Jubilee."

1.7 D. $5.

Not only was Hull worth the big contract (70 goals/39 assists/109 total points in 1991–92), but the Blues raised gate revenues by $3.5 million a year thanks to the $5 ticket hike.

1.8 B. "Three Blind Mice."

In the 1950s this children's ditty was a favourite among arena organists, who could stir the crowd by piping out "Three Blind Mice" whenever the three on-ice officials had, in the organist's opinion, called a bad play against the home team.

1.9 B. Bruins veteran Ted Green.

After being deeked out of his drawers on several occasions at Orr's first Bruins practice, bruising all-star defenseman Green looked ready to go nose-to-nose with the deft rookie who had turned him into a pretzel on the ice. Instead, Green — who knew greatness when he saw it — paid Orr the compliment. It was more appropriate than Green may have realized, considering Orr's landmark contract had made him the NHL's highest-paid rookie. Indeed, whatever Orr got, it was not enough.

1.10 B. The wife of Canada's governor general.

A true upper-crust Briton, Lady Evelyn, wife of Canada's 12th governor general, Baron Byng of Vimy, loved the "Canadian game" but not Canadian fans, whom she regarded as "childish" for showering the rink with garbage and coins to show their displeasure with referees and players. Perhaps that's why she donated a trophy in 1925 to reward the most gentlemanly player in the game.

1.11 A. Maple Leafs owner Harold Ballard.

After being pressed by Coach Neilson to trade Turnbull, a stubborn Ballard made it clear that his favourite defenseman was untouchable, even if the Almighty Himself were available. One clever soul piped back: "How about God and a fourth-round draft choice?"

1.12 C. Policeman.

Until he accepted head coaching duties in 1988, Burns was a full-time cop in Hull, Quebec, by day and coach of the Hull Olympiques by night. Hockey aside, Burns sings C&W in public when the fancy strikes him.

GAME 1

HOMETOWN BOYS

They come from small Canadian towns like Calahoo, Oxbow, Ajax and Trois-Rivières; from Amoka, Ipswich, Chula Vista and other American communities. The NHL displays the world's best hockey because it draws the best players from around the globe, whether they are Texans, Taiwanese, Europeans, Koreans or North American Indians.

Match the players with their hometowns.

(Answers to multiple-choice games are at the back of the book.)

Part 1

1. _____	Belfast, Northern Ireland	a. Al MacInnis
2. _____	Inverness, Nova Scotia	b. Pat Lafontaine
3. _____	Pskow, Commonwealth of	c. Claude Vilgrain
	Independent States	d. Owen Nolan
4. _____	Port-au-Prince, Haiti	e. Sergei Fedorov
5. _____	St. Louis, Missouri	f. Esa Tikkanen
6. _____	Stockport, England	g. Steve Thomas
7. _____	Helsinki, Finland	

Part 2

1. _____	Jakobstad, Sweden	a. Steve Smith
2. _____	Corpus Christi, Texas	b. Tomas Sandstrom
3. _____	Formosa, Taiwan	c. Jim Paek
4. _____	Glasgow, Scotland	d. Petr Klima
5. _____	Maniwaki, Quebec	e. Gino Odjick
6. _____	Chaomotov, Czechoslovakia	f. Brian Leetch
7. _____	Seoul, Korea	g. Rod Langway

LAMPLIGHTERS AND OTHER LEGENDS

In hockey's storied past, goal-scorers were sometimes called "lamplighters," a reference to the goal light or lamp. They played the game with that intensity and passion which, for a brief shining moment, can make the difference between victory and defeat. The lamplighters were men of colourful character; some went on to become Hall of Fame legends, whereas others are remembered for their competitive spirit and brawn.

(Answers are at the end of the chapter.)

2.1 Who was known as "The Babe Ruth of Hockey"?

A. Gordie Howe
B. Howie Morenz
C. Eddie Shore
D. Aurèle Joliat

2.2 The seventh position on early hockey teams was:

A. Rover
B. Point
C. Cover Point
D. Rearguard

2.3 Who was shortest?

A. Cecil "Tiny" Thompson
B. Roy "Shrimp" Worters
C. Harry "Pee-Wee" Oliver
D. Wilfred "Shorty" Green

2.4 How did Hall of Fame goalie Paddy Moran disrupt opposing players' concentration around the net?

A. By cursing them in Gaelic
B. By spitting tobacco
C. By singing "When Irish Eyes Are Smiling"
D. By butt-ending them

2.5 How much ice time do first-line players average per game today compared with 75 years ago?

A. Today: 25 min. vs. 1917: 40 min.
B. Today: 25 min. vs. 1917: 50 min.
C. Today: 30 min. vs. 1917: 50 min.
D. Today: 30 min. vs. 1917: 60 min.

2.6 When Senators goalie Clint Benedict told teammate King Clancy, "Here, kid. Take care of this place till I get back," where was "this place"?

A. The goal net
B. The penalty box
C. A seat in the bar car after winning the Cup
D. The players' bench

2.7 On a per-game basis, what hockey player earned more money in 1910 than baseball's great Ty Cobb?

A. Odie Sprague
B. "Phantom" Joe Malone
C. Fred "Cyclone" Taylor
D. "Newsy" Lalonde

2.8 Who were Ollie Rocco and Lorne Chabotsky?

A. The NHL's first European try-outs in the 1940s
B. The first two bearded NHLers
C. The bogus names of two Rangers players
D. The founders of Canada's first pro hockey league, the Ontario Professional League

2.9 How did Toronto owner Conn Smythe raise money to obtain the great King Clancy from the old Ottawa Senators?

A. He sold the rights to Busher Jackson.
B. He bet on a race horse.
C. He solicited donations at home games.
D. He sold hockey pencils on street corners.

2.10 How many overtime goals did Mel "Sudden Death" Hill *really* score?

A. None — "Sudden Death" was a goalie.
B. Two seventh-game winners
C. Three game-winners in a best-of-seven series
D. Three game-winners in three straight playoffs

2.11 Despite his managerial wizardry, which brought the likes of Charlie Conacher and Ted Kennedy to the Maple Leafs, Frank Selke quit the club in 1946. Why?

A. The Canadiens offered him a better deal.
B. To build an arena in Cincinnati
C. To manage the Ontario Hockey Association
D. He had a falling-out with Leaf owner Conn Smythe.

2.12 He was called "Mr. Zero," but Frank Brimsek is better known for modifying what piece of goalie equipment?

A. The chest protector
B. The stick-hand glove
C. The first leather face mask
D. The goalie jock

2.13 Which Toronto Maple Leaf entered federal politics, became a Member of Parliament and went on to win a Stanley Cup?

A. Bucko McDonald
B. Red Kelly
C. Howie Meeker
D. Lionel Conacher

2.14 Which two NHLers were the last active players from the six-team era? (Guess the year they retired.)

A. Carol Vadnais
B. Jean Ratelle
C. Dave Keon
D. Wayne Cashman

LAMPLIGHTERS AND OTHER LEGENDS
Answers

2.1 B. Howie Morenz.

American sportswriters nicknamed Morenz "The Babe Ruth of Hockey." He was the NHL's first real superstar, a player of unparalleled speed who drew audiences to arenas and brought fans to their feet during his headlong rushes. In the 1920s he racked up totals of 40 goals in 44 games in one season and 30-in-30 in another. But statistics do little to describe the thrill of watching Morenz, the box-office attraction who truly was hockey's Babe Ruth.

2.2 A. Rover.

The rover, considered a fourth forward, was the key man on any club. He was the best skater and all-round player, picking up a drop pass or rebound on the attack and returning to backcheck or bodycheck an opposing puck carrier. The rover was dropped in 1910, not to "open up the game" but for a basic economic reason: it was less expensive to ice six men.

2.3 B. Roy "Shrimp" Worters.

The Shrimp was only 5' 2", but height is no indication of stature. Worters was the first NHL goalie to win the Hart Trophy as League MVP and is one of only four netminders so honoured; "Pee-Wee" Oliver came up big in the Bruins' first Stanley Cup, 1928–29; and "Shorty" Green, as captain of the Hamilton Tigers, staged the NHL's first strike in 1925. As for "Tiny" Thompson, he was actually 5'10". In 12 seasons, he won four Vezinas and zeroed the opposition 81 times, ranking fourth-best in all-time shutouts. Tiny, Shrimp, Pee-Wee and Shorty were anything but small fry; all are Hockey Hall of Fame members.

2.4 B. By spitting tobacco.

Paddy loved his tobacco and chawed it even while tending goal. The habit added another dimension to his game: it wasn't uncommon for opponents in the slot to get an eyeful of Paddy's home brew. Regarded as one of the game's great stand-up specialists, he led the Quebec Bulldogs to Stanley Cups in 1912 and 1913.

2.5 D. Today: 30 min. vs. 1917: 60 min.

Today's first-line player averages about 30 minutes of ice time. Some snipers like Jeremy Roenick or Steve Yzerman play longer, but even they can't best the ironmen who played 60 full minutes in the early days when there were only seven players per team. Line shifts shortened as rosters grew, providing players with fresh legs to speed up the play.

2.6 A. The goal net.

Clancy is probably the only NHLer ever to play every position — including goalie — in one game. In Game Two of the 1923 Ottawa–Edmonton Cup finals, Clancy was recruited to replace hurting defensive stars Buck Boucher and Eddie Gerard, winded centre Frank Nighbor, injured left winger Cy Denneny and exhausted right winger Punch

Broadbent. But Clancy's substituting role didn't end there; in the game's final 10 minutes, goalie Benedict drew a penalty and was forced to serve it in the box. Out skated Clancy again, met by Benedict, who passed on his stick and the famous line about taking care of "this place."

2.7 C. Fred "Cyclone" Taylor.

Taylor signed with the Renfrew Creamery Kings of the National Hockey Association for the astonishing sum of $5,000. In hockey's early years, with many pro leagues competing for survival, signing the best players not only kept teams afloat but ensured the solvency of entire leagues. What we call "franchise" players today were once "league" players. "Cyclone" had that kind of impact, pacing the Ottawa Senators to the 1909 Stanley Cup. In a 12-game season schedule, his $5,000 salary worked out to $416 per game — about 10 times that of baseball's premier player, Ty Cobb.

2.8 C. The bogus names of two Rangers players.

When the Rangers hit Broadway in 1926, sports heroes like Babe Ruth and Jack Dempsey ruled New York. The competition for press coverage was so fierce that Rangers GM Lester Patrick called on Johnny Bruno, a Garden press agent who knew a lot about the publicity game but little of ice hockey. After scanning the Rangers roster for names that would appeal to New York's large ethnic community, Bruno invented Italian winger "Ollie Rocco" and "Lorne Chabotsky," a hot Jewish netminder. These, of course, were bogus names for Oliver Reinikka (of Finnish origin) and Lorne Chabot (who was French-Canadian). The angle was quickly dropped (as was Bruno) when Patrick came across the phoney names in the morning paper.

2.9 B. He bet on a race horse.

Acquiring Clancy was considered the biggest player deal of the 1930s, and Smythe did it with the help of his $250 filly named Rare Jewel — a horse that rarely paid off. One afternoon at the track, Smythe was about to hedge his bets by placing $60 on the race favourite when a former employee teased him about the wager. Without hesitation, the irascible Smythe placed the $60 on his own horse. In the home stretch, Rare Jewel crossed the field and stole the race. Smythe pocketed about $15,000, enough to make up the difference needed to buy King Clancy for $35,000 from the Senators.

2.10 C. Three game-winners in a best-of-seven series.

The Bruins' Mel Hill earned the handle "Sudden Death" the hard way. In the tough-fought Boston–New York semi-finals in 1939, Hill scored three overtime goals in seven games. Even though "Sudden Death" would play on three Stanley Cup winners in his career, he never scored another overtime goal. His NHL record stands today. Not even The Great One, The Rocket or Super Mario has achieved what "Sudden Death" Hill accomplished in seven playoff games back in 1939.

2.11 D. He had a falling-out with Leaf owner Conn Smythe.

Selke made a trade for Montreal's Ted Kennedy without telling Smythe — a breach of discipline, according to the Toronto owner, who was serving in Europe when the deal was made. Ironically, Smythe lucked out. Kennedy potted the 1947 Cup-winner, defeating — you guessed it — Selke's Habs in six games. (Selke had intended to go to Cincinnati but took a "temporary" job in Montreal, where he stayed on to build hockey's greatest dynasty.)

2.12 B. The stick-hand glove.

As a rookie, Brimsek notched six shutouts in seven games, good enough to make Bruins fans tag him "Mr. Zero" and forget their Vezina hero, Tiny Thompson. But Brimsek is remembered for being the first goalie to modify his stick-glove into a blocker so that he could stop shots with the back of his hand.

2.13 B. Red Kelly.

Although all four Leafs served terms as Canadian MPs, only Kelly continued to play hockey during his political career, winning a Cup *after* retiring from the political arena. Kelly, a Liberal, defeated none other than Alan Eagleson, a Progressive Conservative candidate in Canada's 1963 federal election.

2.14 A. Carol Vadnais and D. Wayne Cashman.

Vadnais and Cashman, the last "original six" players, retired in 1982–83 after spending a combined 34 seasons in the NHL. In their 17-year careers, each won two Cups, sharing the Bruins' 1972 championship as teammates. Keon hung up the blades in 1982 after four cups and 18 seasons with Toronto and Hartford. Twenty-one-year veteran Ratelle, who never won the Big One, quit in 1981. Vadnais and Cashman's retirement marked the end of a hockey era.

THE FIRST LINE

The scoring line. Coaches lie awake at night searching for that perfect combination of cornerman, playmaker and sniper. Hockey's greatest teams mastered this balance of talent to produce first-rate lines, some with special names — The Kid Line, The Punch Line and The G-A-G Line. Players on these lines often had their best years together, setting records that stand today.

Fill in the blanks with the missing linemates listed below.

(Answers are at the back of the book.)

Vladimir Krutov	Charlie Conacher
Jacques Lemaire	Rod Gilbert
Marcel Dionne	Gordie Howe
Ted Lindsay	Vic Hadfield
Igor Larionov	Charlie Simmer
Gilbert Perrault	Busher Jackson
Guy Lafleur	Elmer Lach
Toe Blake	René Robert

Left Wing	Centre	Right Wing

1. Detroit's Production Line:

_____ SID ABEL _____

2. Buffalo's French Connection:

RICK MARTIN _____ _____

3. Toronto's Kid Line:

_____ JOE PRIMEAU _____

4. The Soviet K-L-M Line:

_____ _____ SERGEI MAKAROV

5. Montreal's Punch Line:

_____ _____ MAURICE RICHARD

6. The New York Rangers' G-A-G Line:

_____ JEAN RATELLE _____

7. Los Angeles's Triple Crown Line:

DAVE TAYLOR _____ _____

8. Montreal's Dynasty Line:

STEVE SHUTT _____ _____

CHAPTER

3

SWEATERS OF EVERY STRIPE

It's time to suit up and break sweat. This next quiz challenges you with questions about team sweaters, their crests, colours and stripes. Jerseys tell a team's history and show off the names, numbers and captaincy of its members. The questions are straightforward, but don't let the wool be pulled over your eyes.

(Answers are at the end of the chapter.)

3.1 Which symbol appears most often on NHL team crests?

A. Hockey stick
B. Triangle
C. Circle
D. Puck

3.2 Why did Rocket Richard choose No. 9 for his jersey?

A. He had no choice; No. 9 was assigned to him.
B. As a tribute to Gordie Howe's No. 9
C. His newborn daughter weighed nine pounds.
D. No. 9 was his first jersey number in city league.

3.3 When did Wayne Gretzky first start tucking the right side of his hockey sweater into his pants?

A. In Brantford atom league
B. With the Toronto Young Nationals in Junior B
C. With the Soo Greyhounds in Junior A
D. After he won his first Oilers' Cup

3.4 Why does Pittsburgh's Jaromir Jagr wear No. 68?

A. He wanted a number close to Lemieux's No. 66.
B. To commemorate the 1968 Soviet invasion of Czechoslovakia
C. He was born on February 15, 1968.
D. He scored 68 points in his first season with Kladno, his junior Czech team.

3.5 Toronto's No. 6 jersey, worn by the great Ace Bailey, was retired in the 1930s, unretired in the 1960s, and retired again. Why?

A. To comply with an old Harold Ballard policy
B. Another Leafs player wanted No. 6.
C. The Leafs ran short of sweater numbers.
D. Bailey wanted another Leaf to wear No. 6.

3.6 Why did Darryl Sittler cut the captain's "C" off his sweater in 1979–80?

A. He wanted out of his no-trade contract
B. Because he was put on recallable waivers
C. Because of the Lanny MacDonald trade
D. To protest the return of coach Punch Imlach

3.7 Why does Alexander Mogilny wear No. 89?

A. He defected in 1989.
B. He escaped on Flight 89 from Stockholm.
C. He was drafted 89th overall by Buffalo.
D. No. 89 is Mogilny's address in Amherst, N.Y.

3.8 Which hometown fans wear white to playoff games to match their players' sweaters?

A. Washington
B. Winnipeg
C. Vancouver
D. Quebec

3.9 How many jersey numbers did Bobby Hull wear with Chicago?

A. 1
B. 2
C. 3
D. 4

3.10 Who suggested using No. 99 to Wayne Gretzky?

A. Wayne's father
B. Wayne's hockey hero, Gordie Howe
C. Wayne's junior coach, Muzz MacPherson
D. Nelson Skalbania, owner of the WHA Indianapolis Racers

3.11 Toronto owner Harold Ballard made headlines by doing what in 1977?

A. Replacing the old Leaf crest with a more stylized emblem
B. Camouflaging players' names on sweaters
C. Changing the double stripe on the sleeve to a triple stripe to match the socks
D. Removing the small maple leaf on the shoulder

3.12 What NHL team has retired the most jersey numbers?

A. Toronto Maple Leafs
B. Philadelphia Flyers
C. Boston Bruins
D. Montreal Canadiens

3.13 If "C" on sweaters means "Captain," what does "A" stand for?

A. Assistant Captain
B. Associate Captain
C. Alternate Captain
D. Affiliate Captain

3.14 Why did teams begin wearing different sweaters for home and away games?

A. The away sweaters had names on the back.
B. To make teams easier to distinguish on television
C. It was an NHL publicity move.
D. Some teams had similar-coloured uniforms.

3.15 The Chicago Blackhawks have retired only four jersey numbers since joining the NHL in 1926. Which player was honoured first?

A. Glenn Hall
B. Bobby Hull
C. Stan Mikita
D. Tony Esposito

SWEATERS OF EVERY STRIPE
Answers

3.1 C. Circle.
Prominent circles embellish 11 team logos, those of the Senators, Lightning, Oilers, Red Wings, Jets, Canucks, Sabres, Bruins, Flyers, Islanders and Devils. Sticks are another favourite, blazoned on the crests of the Nordiques, Sharks, Jets, Islanders and Capitals. The 24 NHL team logos also display four pucks, three triangles, two skates and one centurion. Lettering is very popular; all but five crests have some alphabetic characters.

3.2 C. His newborn daughter weighed nine pounds.
Although many stars of the 1930s wore No. 9, it wasn't until The Rocket that "9" became hockey's most famous and requested number. Richard began his career in 1942 wearing No. 15, but after daughter Huguette was born, he switched to match her weight. She was truly the apple of her famous father's eye.

3.3 A. In Brantford atom league.

Ever since he began playing hockey at age six, Gretzky has tucked his sweater. Wayne was a little guy in a league for 10-year-olds, and the big sweater kept catching the butt end of his stick; Walter Gretzky tried the simplest solution. Even today Gretzky uses Velcro to make sure his "sweater-tuck" stays put.

3.4 B. To commemorate the 1968 Soviet invasion of Czecho-slovakia.

Born in 1972, Jagr chose a number symbolizing his country's struggle for freedom from communist repression. Ironically, his appearance on draft day in 1990 marked the first time a Czech player attended an NHL draft without having to defect.

3.5 D. Bailey wanted another Leaf to wear No. 6.

After 30 years, Toronto's No. 6 was unretired by Bailey himself, who offered it to Ron Ellis as a tribute to the winger's steady play. Ellis felt so honoured that he wore the famous No. 6 for the next 12 years. When Ellis quit in 1981, the Maple Leafs retired No. 6 again.

3.6 C. Because of the Lanny MacDonald trade.

Not only was Macdonald the fans' most popular player, he and Sittler were linemates and best friends. In protest, Sittler renounced his captaincy by cutting the "C" off his jersey. Considered one of Imlach's worst trades, the deal (MacDonald and Joel Quenneville to the Rockies for Wilf Paiement and Pat Hickey) hurt Sittler personally and cut off his team support. Later, Leaf boss Harold Ballard made peace with his star captain, returning the "C" while Imlach was in hospital.

3.7 A. He defected in 1989.

Considered the best young prospect in the Soviet system, Mogilny was the key to the Red Army team for years. While attending the World Championships in Sweden, he met with Sabres officials, who spirited him out of the country. The cloak-and-dagger operation went more smoothly than expected, but his defection caused a major diplomatic flap. By fluke or by fate, Buffalo drafted Mogilny 89th overall in 1988.

3.8 B. Winnipeg.

Other teams have tried it, but Winnipeg fans have backed the "wear white" campaign 100 percent since it began in 1986. Come playoff time, arena stands are whitewashed in T-shirts, hats and painted faces and hair to cheer on the Jets. The campaign has also helped merchandising, boosting sales 50 percent over regular-season levels.

3.9 C. 3.

Bobby Hull wore Chicago's No. 16 and No. 7 before picking No. 9. He switched because of two other No. 9s — Gordie Howe and Rocket Richard.

3.10 C. Wayne's junior coach, Muzz MacPherson.

The inspiration for No. 99 came when Gretzky was 16 years old and in the OHA. Phil Esposito and Ken Hodge had just been traded to New York. Espo's lucky No. 7 was already being worn by Rod Gilbert, so he took No. 77, and Hodge No. 88. On that cue, MacPherson proposed doubling the "9" of Gordie Howe, Gretzky's hero. On his first night, No. 99 scored two goals. Call it destiny.

3.11 B. Camouflaging players' names on sweaters.

Ballard refused to comply with an NHL rule requiring all teams to display players' names on the backs of their sweaters. Ballard figured sales of player programs would drop. In protest, he had blue letters sewn on the Leafs' blue uniforms, making it impossible to read the names. The stunt lasted one game.

3.12 C. Boston Bruins.

As of 1992, the Bruins have retired seven numbers, including Eddie Shore's No. 2, Bobby Orr's No. 4 and Phil Esposito's No. 7. The Canadiens have retired six numbers, the Flyers four and the Leafs two. No doubt others will soon be added to the list.

3.13 C. Alternate Captain.

Teams have often played for years with alternate captains, choosing not to name a full captain for a variety of reasons. From 1967 to 1973, the Bruins had no "C"s, relying on Esposito, Orr and Bucyk as alternates. This was coach Harry Sinden's way of making every player a leader on the ice.

3.14 B. To make teams easier to distinguish on television.

In the thirties, when Detroit played Montreal, their nearly identical red uniforms made it difficult to distinguish one team from the other, so the visitors wore white pullovers over their game sweaters. But it wasn't until the advent of television that teams adopted two different sweaters, white for away games and coloured for home games. The contrasting uniforms made things easier for television viewers, most of whom had black and white sets. The policy was later reversed so that visiting clubs wore the coloured uniforms.

3.15 C. Stan Mikita.

Mikita's No. 21 was the first number retired in Hawk history (1980), and deservedly so. Whereas others jumped to the WHA, Mikita stayed, saying, "Once a Blackhawk, always a Blackhawk." Hull's famous No. 9 was retired in 1983; Hall's No. 1 and Esposito's No. 35 were retired in a 1988 ceremony honouring both goalies.

CROSSWORD #1

HOCKEY TRIVIA

(Answers to crosswords are at the back of the book.)

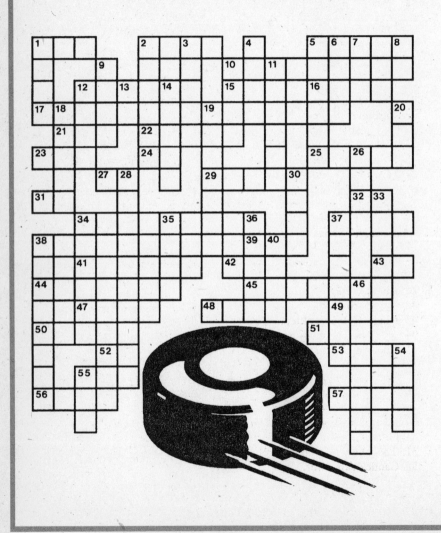

Across

1. Famous N.Y. arena, init.
2. ____-to-back wins
5. _____ box
10. Ex-Oiler, Lee _____ (7 ltrs.)
12. 3-time Norris winner, Hawk's Pierre _____
15. "We ____ the Champions" (3 ltrs.)
16. Ex-Oiler/Bruin goalie, 1st name
17. How to win the game (phrase, 4 wrds., with 26 down)
21. _____ Brind'Amour
22. Misplay
23. ____ plane dive
24. WHA's _____ Whalers, init.
25. Number of Norris's for Orr
27. Hawk No. 7, init.
29. _____ & finesse game
31. Cough ____ the puck
32. ____ MacInnis
34. Take away puck
37. Cherry's dog
38. Opposite of amateur (3 ltrs.)
39. _____ the contract
41. Flyer colour
42. "_____-time it"
43. Kings' Calder rookie, init.
44. _____ before shooting (3 ltrs.)
45. Cheap goal scorer, _____ man
47. _____ strength
48. "_____legs, slow fist"
49. A _____ position
50. Last defenseman to win Hart (3 ltrs.)
51. Too many ____ on the ice
52. Canuck capt., init.
53. _____ the play
56. All-_____
57. Cherry's name for Bruins: Lunch _____ A.C.

Down

1. ____ Sundin
2. 1st U.S. 100-pt. player
3. To applaud
4. _____ ligaments
5. Won 7 Vezinas
6. Stanley Cup _____
7. Up _____
8. Cdn. Olympic goalie, init.
9. Robinson, "Big _____"
10. _____ play
11. "_____man Joe" Primeau
12. _____ judgement
13. Jean Beliveau, "____ Gros Bill"
14. _____ star selection
18. Flame's Stanley Cup coach
19. Gumper
20. ____trick
26. See 17 across.
28. Rookie playoff point record, Dino _____
30. _____ Graham
33. 1st Oiler playoff goal ever, Dave _____
34. Old term for a hard shot
35. Net
36. Smythe Div. team
37. 1st goal, ice _____
38. Post-season
40. Fancy or _____ move
46. Lindros's Jr. team
54. Ex-Jet capt., 1st name
55. Sabres sniper, 1st name

WHO *WAS* THAT MASKED MAN?

They stand padded and masked beyond recognition, rocking between the posts, ready for the inevitable headlong rush, crease scramble or blistering 90-mph boomer. Their judge and jury is a simple red line drawn to distinguish a save from a goal, a win from a loss, and a championship from anything else. It's a bizarre way to make a living. For them, the puck stops here.

(Answers are at the end of the chapter.)

4.1 Which goalie has the most wins in one season?

    A. Bernie Parent
    B. Terry Sawchuk
    C. Ed Belfour
    D. Grant Fuhr

4.2 Which veteran goalie never lost more than 10 games in a season?

    A. Frank Brimsek
    B. Ken Dryden
    C. Jacques Plante
    D. Billy Smith

4.3 How many stitches had been sewn into Jacques Plante's face before the veteran donned hockey's first goalie mask?

A. 100
B. 200
C. 300
D. 400

4.4 When he played the game, they called him the best "money goalie" in the League. Who is he?

A. Turk Broda
B. Tiny Thompson
C. Emile Francis
D. Johnny Bower

4.5 Who was the last goalie captain?

A. Harry Lumley of the Red Wings
B. Bill Durnan of the Canadiens
C. Eddie Johnston of the Bruins
D. Emile Francis of the Blackhawks

4.6 Who holds the record for most shutouts in one season?

A. George Hainsworth
B. Tony Esposito
C. Terry Sawchuk
D. Ken Dryden

4.7 What is the highest number of shots faced by a goalie in a single NHL game?

A. 63
B. 73
C. 83
D. 93

4.8 Who was the first butterfly-type goalie?

A. Glenn Hall
B. Tony Esposito
C. Terry Sawchuk
D. Georges Vezina

4.9 Who was the last maskless NHL goaltender?

A. Cesare Maniago
B. Ed Giacomin
C. Andy Brown
D. Gump Worsley

4.10 What is the most points recorded by a goalie in one season?

A. 6
B. 7
C. 8
D. 14

4.11 Which goalie has the longest undefeated streak?

A. Grant Fuhr
B. Pete Peeters
C. Chico Resch
D. Gerry Cheevers

WHO *WAS* THAT MASKED MAN?
Answers

4.1 A. Bernie Parent.
After Terry Sawchuk set the season record at 44 wins in the early 1950s, two decades of hockey passed before his record was broken. Parent's electrifying 47 season-wins set in 1973-74 still stands, unsuccessfully challenged by Fuhr (40 wins) and Belfour (43 wins). Parent was unequalled in those years, winning 44 games the following season,

1974–75. He took home consecutive Conn Smythes as playoff MVP, two Stanley Cups and double Vezinas.

4.2 B. Ken Dryden.

In eight seasons with Montreal, Dryden led the League in victories four times, won the Vezina five times and the Stanley Cup six times and never lost more than 10 games per season. In *The Game*, the ever-humble Dryden says: "On a team as good as the Canadiens . . . I get fewer shots, and fewer hard shots; I must allow fewer goals, the teams I play on must win Stanley Cups. Most envy my job, some are not so sure."

4.3 B. 200.

When Plante introduced the mask in 1959, pucks, sticks, elbows and skates had carved up his face, his nose had been broken four times, his jaw and both cheekbones had been fractured and he had sustained a hairline skull fracture. Even so, critics (including goalies) called him puck-shy. Facial injuries were normal, a trademark in an occupation full of hazards. Plante won the next 11 games with his mask on, yet coaches remained skeptical, concerned about restricted vision. The most scarred goalie was probably Terry Sawchuk, who took 400 stitches in his face, including three in the right eyeball. He waited until 1962 before donning a mask.

4.4 A. Turk Broda.

Among the old-timers, Broda was considered the best at backstopping the "big" games. In 14 seasons with Toronto, he took the Leafs to five Cups, including the 1942 come-from-behind classic against Detroit. With Toronto down three games to none, Broda allowed only seven goals in the last four games. His lifetime goals-against average? Regular season: 2.53; playoffs: 1.98. Broda was the best "money goalie" around. As one hockey man said, in the playoffs: "He could catch lint in a hurricane."

4.5 B. Bill Durnan of the Canadiens.

Goalie captains are a rarity — since 1917, only five NHL netminders have captained teams. Durnan was the last, wearing the "C" from 1946 to 1948. His career spanned only seven seasons, but in that time Durnan was awarded the Vezina six times, played on six All-Star teams and won the Stanley Cup twice. He was a true leader on a team of Richards, Lachs and Blakes. Goalies Lumley, Johnston and Francis never captained.

4.6 A. George Hainsworth.

Few can challenge Hainsworth's record of 22 shutouts in 1928–29. He allowed just 43 goals in a 44-game schedule, for an incredible goals-against average of 0.98. His shutout mark is unlikely to be surpassed, although Tony Esposito came close with 15 shutouts in 63 games in 1969–70.

4.7 C. 83.

In 1941, Chicago goalie Sam LoPresti took it on the chin and every other part of his anatomy in a puck barrage that swamped him with 83 shots — a record unequalled to this day. The pucks came from every conceivable angle as the Blackhawks were hard-pressed to clear their zone. Despite the Bruin onslaught, LoPresti allowed just three goals . . . but lost the game 3–2.

4.8 A. Glenn Hall.

Unlike the classic "stand-up" goalie, Hall positioned his legs wide apart. His spread-eagle style, the "butterfly," covered more area between the posts, providing better manoeuvrability against deflections and rebounds. The unorthodox crouch served him well. In 16 seasons, he iced 64 shutouts — the third-best shutout record ever. His "butterfly" became a standard for goalies like Tony Esposito and Patrick Roy.

4.9 C. Andy Brown.

A journeyman goalie, Brown staked his claim to fame in his last NHL game as a Penguin on March 31, 1973. The maskless goalie was henceforth extinct (although Brown continued to play barefaced with the WHA Indianapolis Racers). Gump Worsley's contempt for the mask is well known. He was the last goalie of his generation to go barefaced, yielding only in his final season — 14 years after Jacques Plante first wore a mask in 1959.

4.10 D. 14.

Everyone on the Oilers scored big-time in 1983–84, including Grant Fuhr, who chalked up a record 14 points, all in assists. Closest to Fuhr in season points: Mike Palmateer and Ron Hextall, with 8 points each.

4.11 D. Gerry Cheevers.

Cheevers's streak of 32 games (24 wins–8 ties) without a loss in 1971–72, during the Bruins's Stanley Cup years, is unequalled by any other netminder, but one goalie did manage to make it interesting. In 1982–83, Peeters reached 31 games (26 wins–5 ties) before losing the game that would have tied the record. Resch and Fuhr each have 15 wins–8 ties.

CROSSWORD #2

GOALIES

(Answers to crosswords are at the back of the book.)

Across

2. _____ hands with puck
4. _____ Pietrangelo
6. _____ Jose
10. Camille "The ____" Henry
12. 1991 Vezina, 1st name
15. Scored on _____ (2 wrds., 8 ltrs.)
19. Goalie glove (7 ltrs.)
20. Ken Linseman's nickname
21. _____ Mantha, ex-Canuck
24. _____out
26. _____ing the puck out of the air
28. Rookie trophy
29. Montreal _____, 1st Cup Champs, 1893
30. Coach called Captain Video, init. (2 ltrs.)
31. Shooting position next to crease
33. "_____ of defeat"
35. "____ to ____" (with 53 Down)
37. _____ coverage
39. Cam Neely is a _____
42. In alone
44. Elmer Vasco nickname
46. _____ Giacomin
47. Part of net, abbrv.
48. "The Rocket," init.
49. _____-hander (3 ltrs.)
51. Goal _____
54. ____ward
55. Kings's No. 16 (6 ltrs.)
56. "Cement Hands" (5 ltrs.)
59. Ex-Leaf winger, init.
60. _____ Cheveldae
61. Penguin Czech.
63. Ted Kennedy nickname
64. "_____ down the angle"

Down

1. Net area
2. To block view
3. Esa Tikkanen nickname
5. League initials (3 ltrs.)
7. Empty _____ goal
8. _____ goal
9. Shutout number
11. Messier's hometown
13. Goalie with most Stanley Cups
14. "He's a good _____"
16. To shout
17. Extra period, abbrv.
18. Jim _____linski, ex-Flame
22. "Perfect score"
23. Net action
25. Dave Taylor's team
27. Wing's only Conn Smythe winner
32. Phil's "kid brother," init.
34. Extra period
36. Disallowed goal: "____ goal"
38. "_____ Dog" Kelly (3 ltrs.)
39. _____ formation
40. To steal a goal from scorer
41. 1980 Olympic gold medal–winning country, init.
43. Famous Maple Leaf from 1960s
45. 1970 & 1975 scoring leader
48. Traded to Boston for Courtnall & Ranford
50. Sher-_____
51. Rick Tabaracci is a _____
52. _____ and chase
53. See 35 Across.
57. _____ Fontinato
58. Devils's U.S. state, init.
62. Forward position, init.

IN WHAT YEAR . . . ?

It wasn't so long ago that the NHL first instituted a rule whereby the third man to enter a fight was assessed a game misconduct — or was it? In fact, the NHL rule came into effect in 1971. And it seemed like only yesterday . . . This quiz tests your logic and your memory of dates in hockey history.

(Answers are at the end of the chapter.)

5.1 In what year(s) did the Soviets win the Canada Cup?

    A. 1976
    B. 1981
    C. 1984
    D. 1987

5.2 In what year did it become mandatory for NHL teams to put players' names on sweaters?

    A. 1970
    B. 1974
    C. 1977
    D. 1980

5.3 In what year did advertising first appear on NHL-arena rink boards?

A. 1972
B. 1975
C. 1979
D. 1981

5.4 In what year was the Zamboni introduced to hockey? (Name the NHL arena.)

A. 1940
B. 1945
C. 1950
D. 1955

5.5 In what year did an NHLer first use the "reverse grip" (both hands on the same side of the stick) to face off?

A. 1926
B. 1936
C. 1946
D. 1956

5.6 In what year did goalies stop serving penalties in the penalty box?

A. 1920
B. 1930
C. 1940
D. 1950

5.7 In what year was bodily contact on faceoffs prohibited?

A. 1934
B. 1944
C. 1954
D. 1964

5.8 In what year was the first NHL game broadcast on American network TV?

A. 1952
B. 1955
C. 1957
D. 1960

5.9 In what year was the 100-point mark first broken?

A. 1966–67
B. 1967–68
C. 1968–69
D. 1969–70

5.10 In what year was the NHL's 100,000th goal scored?

A. 1962
B. 1972
C. 1982
D. 1992

5.11 In what year was the first goalie pulled to add an extra attacker?

A. 1911
B. 1921
C. 1931
D. 1941

5.12 In what year did Gordie Howe and sons Mark and Marty first play pro hockey on the same line?

A. 1971
B. 1973
C. 1977
D. 1980

5.13 To accommodate the names of the 1992 Stanley Cup champion Penguins, the NHL added another tier to the base of the Cup. In what year will the League run out of space again?

A. 1999
B. 2005
C. 2010
D. 2015

5.14 In what year did the first chartered flight in NHL history take off? (Name the team on board.)

A. 1940
B. 1945
C. 1950
D. 1955

5.15 After topping Gordie Howe's all-time point total in 1989, Wayne Gretzky is poised to break another Howe record: the all-time goal-scoring mark. Gretzky steadily inches closer to the record, having scored 16 goals in 1992–93 for a total of 765 goals. If he scores at least 35 goals per season, in what year will The Great One become the NHL's all-time goal-scoring leader?

A. 1992–93
B. 1993–94
C. 1994–95
D. 1995–96

IN WHAT YEAR . . . ?
Answers

5.1 B. 1981.

The Canada Cup, which brings together the world's best players, has been won by the Soviets only once. After the final game, tournament organizer Alan Eagleson rushed into the Soviet dressing room in search of the Canada Cup trophy, which the Soviet players had stuffed into a duffle bag for the trip home. Host officials had failed to inform participating teams that the trophy stayed in Canada. Months later, an ad hoc group of Canadians made a replica of the Canada Cup and presented it to the Soviet National Team in Moscow.

5.2 C. 1977.

Although the 1928 Brooklyn Americans were the first to do it, it wasn't until 1970 that the NHL instituted a policy allowing home teams to put players' names on uniforms; in 1977, another resolution made it *mandatory* for all clubs, home and away, to display players' names.

5.3 C. 1979.

The first time rink boards were used as advertising space was during the 1979 Challenge Cup, a three-game series between Team NHL and the Soviet National Team at Madison Square Garden. The series, won by the Soviets two games to one, replaced the 1979 NHL All-Star game.

5.4 D. 1955.

Old records indicate that both Boston Garden and the Montreal Forum received Zambonis in 1954. However, the Forum is credited with using its Zamboni first, on March 10, 1955.

5.5 D. 1956.

The "reverse grip" was introduced in a Toronto–Boston game by the Bruins's Jack Caffery on November 18, 1956. For many faceoff men, the reverse hand position gives better leverage in drawing the puck away from the opponent.

5.6 C. 1940.

The 1940–41 season marked the first time a goalie could not be sent to the penalty box for any minor infraction. Prior to this, a substitute "goalie" was appointed — which meant a teammate (always a skater, since there were no spare netminders in those days), who was only allowed to use the penalized goalie's stick and gloves. With the 1940 rule change came an interesting twist: rather than assessing the goalie a penalty, a penalty shot would be awarded to the opposing team.

5.7 D. 1964.

Rule 52(c), eliminating physical contact on the faceoff, came into effect in 1964 after a number of teams began using wingers as faceoff men strictly to take out the opposing centre, rather than playing the puck. The strategy allowed the defending centre to go in unmolested, get the puck and thus gain an unfair advantage.

5.8 C. 1957.

CBS televised the first network game on January 5, 1957. The Rangers beat the Blackhawks 4–1.

5.9 C. 1968–69.

Fifty-two years after the NHL was formed and one season after the 1967 expansion, the 100-point mark was smashed, by not one but three players. Phil Esposito (126), Bobby Hull (107) and Gordie Howe (103) each racked up more points than any NHLer had ever scored before.

5.10 C. 1982.

On March 27, 1982, Quebec's Wilf Paiement scored goal No. 100,000 during a 4–2 Nordiques loss at the Montreal Forum.

5.11 D. 1941.

The first time a net was left undefended to gain extra offense was during a Chicago–Toronto game in 1941. Since it had never been tried before, Chicago coach Paul Thompson pulled goalie Sam LoPresti while his team was already in a man-advantage situation on a Maple Leafs' penalty. Although the Blackhawks failed to score, the tactic made perfect hockey sense and soon became common.

5.12 B. 1973.

In 32 hockey seasons, Gordie Howe's biggest thrill was playing with Mark and Marty. It happened on October 13, 1973, when the Howes took their first shift together as members of the WHA Houston Aeros. When the Aeros folded, the Howe clan joined the New England Whalers and later played their first NHL game together, before Gordie retired in 1980. This was the only time in NHL history that father and son(s) have played together.

5.13 B. 2005.

Finding silver space on Lord Stanley's coveted Cup is becoming a problem. The 1992 champion Penguins are the first team to have their name engraved on the Cup's new tier. Its circumference will accommodate the names of 13 championship teams.

5.14 A. 1940.

The Chicago Blackhawks were the first team to travel by air on a chartered flight. They flew to Toronto on March 18, 1940, for the Stanley Cup finals.

5.15 B. 1993–94.

Game after game, Gretzky comes closer to Howe's record of 801 career goals, which should be broken in 1993–94 if Gretzky scores 37 goals that season.

GAME 3

THE HOCKEY BUILDERS

The following names are well known, but the accomplishments of these hockey personalities may be less familiar. Match the men with their contributions to the game.

(Answers are at the back of the book.)

Jack Adams	Frank Calder
Lord Stanley	Art Ross
Dr. David Hart	Clarence Campbell
James Norris	Conn Smythe
Lester Patrick	William Jennings

1. _____ Built Canada's first artificial ice rink

2. _____ Rangers boss who pioneered the NHL's 1967 expansion to 12 teams

3. _____ Personally responsible for founding the Hockey Hall of Fame

4. _____ Signed and developed Gordie Howe into a superstar

5. _____ Unfortunately, never attended a Stanley Cup game

6. _____ Established the NHL Pension Society

7. _____ Innovator who redesigned the NHL puck and goalie net

8. _____ Owned Chicago Stadium, Madison Square Garden and the Olympia; renamed Detroit club the "Red Wings"

9. _____ First president of the NHL

10. _____ Donated the NHL's oldest individual trophy

CHAPTER

6

RULES AND EQUIPMENT

Each season the game evolves a little to make play more exciting for the spectator. Rules are changed to speed up the game; equipment is designed and developed to protect the players. In this quiz we pit your stick-handling know-how against brainteasers about hockey's rules and equipment.

(Answers are at the end of the chapter.)

6.1 Hockey's penalty shot was derived from what sport?

    A. Soccer
    B. Lacrosse
    C. Polo
    D. Hockey

6.2 Why did the NHL conduct an investigation into goalie nets in 1957?

    A. To verify net size
    B. To prove the netting was "puck-proof"
    C. To check for illegal hemp
    D. To determine the best method for anchoring posts

6.3 Who made Jacques Plante's first goalie mask?

    A. A fibre-glass manufacturer
    B. An unknown fan
    C. NASA
    D. Plante himself

6.4 **Which of these coaches is credited with introducing the three-forward line system?**

A. The Pirates' Odie Cleghorn
B. The Rangers' Lester Patrick
C. The Blackhawks' Dick Irvin
D. The Canadiens' Leo Dandurand

6.5 **What method did referees once use to face off?**

A. The puck was placed on the ice.
B. The puck has always been dropped.
C. The puck was flipped upwards.
D. The puck was tossed into the faceoff circle, and the centres raced to reach it.

6.6 **Which sport inspired hockey's goalie pads?**

A. Shinty
B. Field hockey
C. Cricket
D. Hurley

6.7 **Who first observed the effectiveness of a curved stick blade?**

A. Andy Bathgate
B. Bobby Hull
C. Stan Mikita
D. Cy Denneny

6.8 **Defensemen once lined up behind one another on faceoffs, rather than side by side. What brought about the change?**

A. Canadian football
B. Hockey's seventh position, the rover, was abolished.
C. One defenseman never saw the faceoffs.
D. Too many injuries

6.9 Besides the face mask, which other innovation did Jacques Plante popularize?

A. Thrusting his arm up for icing calls
B. The throat protector
C. The pre-game skate/warm-up
D. Talking to his goal posts

6.10 Which NHLer is responsible for Rule 27(c), which allows a penalized player to return to the ice when a goal is scored by the opposing team?

A. Dickie Moore
B. Henri Richard
C. Bernie Geoffrion
D. Jean Beliveau

6.11 Goalies were fined and penalized prior to 1920 for:

A. Falling down to make a save
B. Wearing oversized pads
C. Kicking the puck out of the crease
D. Raising the stick above shoulder height

6.12 To cut down on net displacements, the NHL replaced net magnets with flexible rubber pegs in 1991–92. Previously, how often per game, on average, would a net dislodge from the magnets?

A. 3 times
B. 6 times
C. 9 times
D. 12 times

6.1 C. Polo.

The penalty shot is one of many innovations introduced to hockey by the famous Patrick brothers. After witnessing a polo match in England, Frank Patrick adapted the rule to suit our sport. The Patricks not only played the game but went on to coach, manage and own a pro league that competed with the NHL for the best players and the Stanley Cup. In the teens and twenties they proposed the playoff concept, the offside rule (by painting blue lines on the ice) and uniform numbers on sweaters.

6.2 A. To verify net size.

Everyone thought Jacques Plante was crazy when he said NHL nets varied in size . . . until measurements were taken. Even though all NHL clubs used official goal nets, Plante believed nets in three rinks (Chicago, Boston and New York) were lower than the 4-foot regulation height. It was soon discovered to be true. Three NHL rinks had welded the 2-inch-thick crossbar to the sides of the posts rather than to their tops, thus shortening the nets by 2 inches in height. Plante noticed the irregularity because the crossbars hit his back at different levels.

6.3 B. An unknown fan.

In 1955, a Forum fan sent Plante a small plastic mask. Even though it obscured his vision, Plante wore it religiously in practices after a puck struck the mask square in an eyehole. Plante's first game mask was made by Fibreglas Canada of woven roping saturated with polyester resin. Don't laugh: NASA's space engineers did consult with Plante in the 1960s.

6.4 A & C. The Pirates' Odie Cleghorn and The Black-hawks' Dick Irvin.

Until the 1920s, teams played with two good lines. Around the time the NHL increased maximum team strength to 14 players, Cleghorn and Irvin changed the offensive tactics of hockey by using three lines in short shifts. Cleghorn's idea of changing players "on the fly" was another offensive manoeuvre that disoriented opponents. Both are standards in hockey today.

6.5 A. The puck was placed on the ice.

Until Fred C. Waghorne came along, faceoffs looked very different. Referees lined up the centres and put the puck between their stick blades, yelling "play" to signal the start of play. Waghorne changed that by simply dropping the puck. He was also the first official to use a whistle instead of a handbell to stop play.

6.6 C. Cricket.

The origins of hockey can be traced back to older games like shinty, field hockey and hurley, but cricket gave us the goalie pad. In an 1896 Stanley Cup game, spectators and players were flabbergasted when Winnipeg goalie George Merritt stepped onto the ice wearing white cricket pads. After some discussion over their legality, the game began and Merritt proved their worth by posting the first shutout in Stanley Cup history.

6.7 A. Andy Bathgate.

Although the annals of hockey include references to Cy Denneny using a curved stick in the 1920s, the credit belongs to Andy Bathgate. In the late 1950s, the Rangers star noticed that a bent blade made his shots jump and dip in flight. Soon after, by chance, Stan Mikita realized the same thing while practising with a stick cracked vertically along the blade. By trial and error, Mikita and teammate Bobby Hull used a simple steaming method to curve their blades.

After some experimentation, they discovered the optimum curvature for adding velocity and accuracy to their blasts. Hockey changed almost overnight. Bathgate knew he was onto something with the bent blade, but Hull and Mikita first realized its full potential.

6.8 A. Canadian football.

Bo Jackson is not the first multi-sport player; long ago, athletes often switched sports in off-seasons. So it wasn't unusual when a few of football's Toronto Argonauts played in the Ontario Hockey Association's 1906 championship game. More surprising to hockey fans of that era was how these defensemen lined up side by side on faceoffs, like defensive linemen in football. Shortly thereafter, the tandem stance (with players behind one another) was dropped and all defensemen aligned themselves an equal distance from the faceoff. Credit the Toronto Argonauts with changing hockey's defense positioning.

6.9 A. Thrusting his arm up for icing calls.

Plante was the first goalie to alert his teammates to icing calls by raising his arm. (By the way, Plante hated the pre-game warm-up. Plante suggested using spares instead, because he felt the extra work took away a goalie's edge before the game. And if Plante did talk to his posts, he wasn't the first.)

6.10 D. Jean Beliveau.

At one time, any player serving a minor penalty spent the full two minutes in the box, no matter what. That changed after a Bruins–Canadiens game on November 5, 1955. With Montreal holding a two-man advantage over Boston, Beliveau swept in on goalie Terry Sawchuk three times to score a hat trick in 44 seconds. Bruins GM Lynn Patrick appealed to League governors, who later enacted a rule whereby penalized teams revert to normal strength if a goal is scored against them.

6.11 A. Falling down to make a save.

Goaltenders were once required to block all shots standing up. Until 1917, if the goalie fell to the ice to make a save or stop the play, he was assessed a minor penalty — or a $2.00 fine! Sprawling goalie Clint Benedict prompted the rule change, although not before he attained some proficiency in "faking it." "If you did it a bit sneaky and made it look accidental, you could fall on the puck without being penalized," he once said. Restrictions on goalie pad width (12 inches) came into effect in 1926.

6.12 B. 6 times.

Before the Marsh flexible peg was adopted, play was stopped an average of six times per game because magnets failed to hold the net in place. Fred Marsh, an ice maker from Kitimat, B.C., invented the 8-inch rubber pegs, which hold the net more securely while still allowing some give to ensure player safety. The net result: with Marsh's pegs, displacements average less than one per game.

ALL-STAR LINES

"I went to a fight and a hockey game broke out" is probably the most-quoted hockey one-liner. But the game's humour, true grit and spirit are expressed far better by those who play, watch and coach the game. They've given us many great sports quotes — along with a few words that are more memorable than inspiring.

Match the poets of the puck with their pithy ponderings.

(Answers are at the back of the book.)

Part 1

Fred Shero   Conn Smythe
Andre Dupont   Jim Schoenfeld
Wayne Gretzky   Wall graffiti

1. _____ "If you can't beat 'em in the alley, you can't beat 'em on the ice."

2. _____ "Jesus saves, but Orr scores on the rebound."

3. _____ "It was a good day for us. We didn't go to jail, we beat up their chicken forwards, we scored goals and we won. Now the Moose drinks beer."

4. _____ "Life is just a place we spend time between games."

(Continues on page 62)

5. _____ "Have another donut, you fat pig!"

6. _____ "Corners are for bus stops and stamps.

Part 2

Bob Johnson	Jacques Plante
Harry Neale	Barclay Plager
Gump Worsley	Don Cherry

1. _____ "It's not the size of the dog in the fight, but the size of the fight in the dog."

2. _____ "Goaltending a normal job? Sure, how would you like it, if every time you made a mistake, a red light went on over your desk and 15,000 people stood up and yelled at you."

3. _____ The tough player's credo: "It's not how many you win; it's how many you show up for."

4. _____ "We're losing at home; we can't win on the road. My failure as a coach is that I can't figure out any place else to play."

5. _____ "Anyone who wears one is chicken."

6. _____ "It's a great day for hockey."

CHAPTER

7

IN THE NUMBERS

Who holds the record for the most short-handed goals scored by a rookie left winger in a playoff game on the road in an 84-game schedule? We're not sure, but this collection of questions adds up to a numerical challenge. Put away the calculators; a little common sense will help you figure it out.

(Answers are at the end of the chapter.)

7.1 On average, how often does the puck change possession each period?

A. About 60 times
B. About 90 times
C. About 120 times
D. About 180 times

7.2 What is the most shots on goal in one season by an NHLer? (He did it in the 1970s.)

A. 250
B. 450
C. 550
D. 750

7.3 Bobby Hull's slapshot is generally considered the fastest of his era. How fast was it?

A. 80 mph
B. 100 mph
C. 120 mph
D. 140 mph

7.4 It was a precedent-setting sum of money to pay a hockey player — even if it was for a top rookie prospect named Bobby Orr. How much was Orr's deal worth in 1966?

A. Less than $100,000
B. $100,000 to $200,000
C. $200,000 to $400,000
D. More than $400,000

7.5 How often has a hockey player or team been voted *Sports Illustrated*'s Sportsman of the Year?

A. Only once
B. 3 times
C. 5 times
D. 7 times

7.6 How many Rangers did Phil Esposito trade in his first season as GM in New York?

A. 16
B. 19
C. 22
D. 25

7.7 Chicago's Steve Larmer was selected in what position overall in the 1980 draft?

A. 30th
B. 60th
C. 90th
D. 120th

7.8 How many knee operations has Bobby Orr had?

A. 9
B. 11
C. 13
D. 15

7.9 What is the highest number of points any NHLer (read: Wayne Gretzky) has scored in one season, *including* playoffs?

A. 225
B. 255
C. 285
D. 325

7.10 What percentage of players voted against regular-season overtime in 1980–81?

A. 50%
B. 66%
C. 85%
D. 100%

7.11 How long was the longest NHL game ever?

A. 5 overtime periods
B. 6 overtime periods
C. 7 overtime periods
D. 8 overtime periods

7.12 At what age did the NHL's oldest rookie enter the League?

A. 30
B. 34
C. 38
D. 42

7.13 In NHL history, how many times have two players (other than Dionne and Gretzky in 1980) tied for the scoring title?

A. Never
B. Only once
C. 4 times
D. 7 times

7.14 How many international games did Canada's Olympic hockey team play in the four years before the 1992 Olympics?

A. 159
B. 209
C. 259
D. 309

7.15 Before the 1992 "optional" helmet ruling, how many players played bareheaded in 1991–92?

A. None
B. 5
C. 10
D. 15

IN THE NUMBERS
Answers

7.1 C. About 120 times.

According to Ken Dryden, the puck changes teams more than six times a minute, or 120 times a period. Dryden says: "Hockey is a transition game: offence to defence, defence to offence, one team to another. . . . The puck is often out of possession, fought after, in no one's control. It's the nature of the game, North American or European. There is sustained possession only on power plays."

7.2 C. 550.

In 1970–71, Phil Esposito blasted 550 shots at netminders, connecting 76 times in the 78-game schedule — an average of seven shots on net per game. No one else has come close. Bobby Hull scored 58 goals in 414 shots in 1968–69, and son Brett had 70 goals in 408 shots in 1991–92.

7.3 C. 120 mph.

Speed tests clocked Hull's shot at 119.5 mph. Ken Dryden and Jacques Plante figured that at that speed a Hull slapshot from the blue line, aimed at the glove-side upper corner, would be impossible to stop. Mathematically, a puck blasted at 120 mph would blaze from stick to net (60 feet) in less than half a second (.352 second), too quick to catch if the goalie's glove hand is 2 feet below the puck entry point. If you blinked on a Hull slapshot, Plante admitted, you would see only a black blur before the puck entered the net or hit you. Incidentally, Hull's wrist shot was measured at 105 mph and his backhand at 96 mph!

7.4 A. Less than $100,000.

It sounds almost ludicrous in today's market of million-dollar deals and rich signing bonuses, but until Orr's landmark contract in 1966, hockey's best rookie was mailed a two-year contract for $10,250, including bonuses! Orr's agent, Alan Eagleson, countered this pittance by hinting his client might join Canada's Olympic team instead of turning pro. After the noise died down, the Bruins dealt a $25,000 bonus, $25,000 in Year One, and $30,000 in Year Two. The player agent had arrived. More important, so had Bobby Orr.

7.5 B. 3 times.

Since the magazine was founded in 1954, *SI* has so honoured Bobby Orr (1970), the gold-medal U.S. Olympic team (1980) and Wayne Gretzky (1982).

7.6 B. 19.

Never one to shun any spotlight, not even Broadway's brightest, Esposito quickly earned the nickname "Trader Phil" in New York by completing 19 player trades in his first season as GM. He also fired or replaced two head coaches before going behind the bench himself.

7.7 D. 120th.

After he scored 114 points in 67 games for the OHA's Niagara Falls Flyers, it's a wonder Larmer wasn't picked earlier in the 1980 draft, especially when you check the choices that year — only Coffey, Savard and Hrudey really stand out. Larmer didn't go until the sixth round, a bargain for the Hawks, who saw their lowly draft pick (5' 11", 175 lb.) turn into the 1983 Rookie of the Year and remain an ironman for 10 full seasons.

7.8 C. 13.

Between 1967 and 1980, Orr's left knee went under the knife 13 times to repair cartilage and ligament damage.

7.9 B. 255.

In 1984–85, Gretzky totalled 208 points in 80 regular-season games, adding 47 points in 18 playoff games.

7.10 C. 85%.

Most NHLers voted against overtime because, points-wise, a tie in regulation time is better than a loss in the extra period.

7.11 B. 6 overtime periods.

At 16:30 of the sixth overtime, after almost nine periods of scoreless hockey, Detroit rookie Mud Bruneteau lifted the puck over sprawling Maroons goalie Lorne Chabot to end the 1936 Cup semi-final classic Detroit 1–Montreal 0. The ice was badly chopped, the players and fans were exhausted, and the dazed goal judge failed to flash the red light indicating a goal. Bruneteau's mark ended the March 24 game at 2:25 A.M. on March 25.

7.12 C. 38.

St. Louis Blues defenseman Connie Madigan became the oldest rookie in NHL history on February 7, 1973, when he played in his first NHL game at the age of 38. His hockey career began in 1955–56 in Thunder Bay, Ontario. Over the next 18 years, Madigan bounced from team to team, playing in three amateur and four semi-pro leagues (WHL, CHL, IHL and AHL) before the big call came from the Blues organization. Madigan played 20 games, earning three assists and 25 penalty minutes. The following season he was back in the WHL with the San Diego Gulls.

7.13 B. Only once.

In 1962, Andy Bathgate and Bobby Hull finished the season with 84 points each. Hull won the Art Ross for having scored more goals.

7.14 C. 259.

Canada's Olympic team played 259 games in the United States, Europe and Japan in preparation for the 26th Winter Olympiad in Albertville, France. They won the silver medal.

7.15 B. 5.

Craig MacTavish, Brad Marsh, Doug Wilson, Randy Carlyle and Rod Langway were the last holdouts from a hockey era when a standard player's contract signed before June 1, 1979 — the date helmets became mandatory in the NHL — was the qualification for exemption. Now that headgear is optional again, helmet doffing fuels the long-argued debate over the risks versus the rewards.

THE NAME OF THE GAME

Let's face it, nicknames aren't as original as they used to be. Gone are the days of "Bullet Joe," "Jake the Snake" and "Mr. Zero." Today, few names capture our imagination, except maybe the Canucks' "Russian Rocket." More interesting are names coined by teammates. Pavel Bure is "Pasha," and Geoff Courtnall is "7–11," because he shouts, "I'm open, I'm open," while on the fly.

Few outsiders know these handles born in dressing rooms and on bus rides. For instance, take the night Winnipeg's Randy Carlyle blind-passed the puck in his own zone to an opponent who, as an ex-teammate, knew "Kitty" was Carlyle's nickname. "Kitty, pass it here." Randy's blind pass was perfect. Right onto the stick of his opponent, who one-timed it to score. Hey, it happens.

Unless we were told, how would we know Paul Cavallini is "Wally" (he reads the *Wall Street Journal)* or Kevin Lowe is "Vish" (he once resembled punker Sid Vicious)? But we might figure out who "Tide" is, if Ron *Lowe* entered the room.

Here are more imaginative spinoffs conjured up by NHLers. Match the players with their nicknames.

(Answers are at the back of the book.)

Part 1

1. _____ Vincent Damphousse   a. Elvis

2. _____ Michel Goulet   b. Psycho

3. _____ Trevor Linden   c. Iggy

4. _____ Jeremy Roenick   d. Muddy

5. _____ Wayne Presley   e. "T"

6. _____ Mike Richter   f. Tabby

7. _____ Vladimir Ruzicka   g. The Vin-Meister

8. _____ Tim Waters   h. Lucky

9. _____ Rick Tabaracci   i. Goo

10. _____ Igor Larionov   j. Rosie

11. _____ Luc Robitaille   k. Ricky

12. _____ Phil Sykes   l. Swede

13. _____ Tomas Sandstrom   m. J. R.

Part 2

1. _____ Grant Fuhr   a. Eddie O

2. _____ Craig Janney   b. Stitch

3. _____ Dave Taylor   c. Simmer

4. _____ Kirk McLean   d. Howie

5. _____ Craig Simpson   e. Charlie

6. _____ Eddie Olczyk   f. Coco

7. _____ Steve Larmer   g. Screwy

8. _____ Dave Manson   h. Gravy

9. _____ Brian Skrudland   i. C. J.

10. _____ Ray Bourque   j. Bubba

11. _____ Tim Cheveldae   k. Gramps

12. _____ Adam Graves   l. Chevy

13. _____ Dale Hawerchuk   m. Mac

CHAPTER 8

THE ICEMEN COMETH

Once every few years a player destined for superstardom breaks into the pro ranks. Bobby Orr, for instance. His blinding talent forever changed the game. Those headlong rushes up-ice altered the way defensemen play their position and brought a new generation of fans to hockey. Pure skill. Finesse. Hockey smarts. This quiz is about the game's greatest stars and superstars. Shoot first and ask questions later.

(Answers are at the end of the chapter.)

8.1 Why didn't Wayne Gretzky win Rookie of the Year?

    A. He was ineligible because he'd been a WHA pro.
    B. His NHL rookie season was unspectacular.
    C. He was runner-up to Boston's Ray Bourque.
    D. He didn't play enough games to be eligible.

8.2 Who holds the record for most points in one game?

    A. Mario Lemieux
    B. Bryan Trottier
    C. Wayne Gretzky
    D. Darryl Sittler

8.3 Who was hockey's first million-dollar player?

A. Phil Esposito
B. Bobby Orr
C. Derek Sanderson
D. Bobby Hull

8.4 When Wayne Gretzky and Marcel Dionne tied the scoring championship in 1980, the Art Ross Trophy was awarded to:

A. The player with the most goals
B. The player with fewer games played
C. The player who scored the first goal of the season
D. Both players

8.5 Which NHLer has never won the Norris Trophy for best defenseman?

A. Rod Langway
B. Brad Park
C. Chris Chelios
D. Doug Wilson

8.6 After Wayne Gretzky, who was the NHL's point leader in the 1980s?

A. Jari Kurri
B. Peter Stastny
C. Denis Savard
D. Paul Coffey

8.7 Of these over-30 veterans, who was the oldest when he scored his first 50-goal season?

A. John Bucyk
B. Joe Mullen
C. Vic Hadfield
D. Lanny MacDonald

8.8 Who is the only player in NHL history to record one of each possible type of goal in a single game?

A. Vincent Damphousse
B. Phil Esposito
C. Brett Hull
D. Mario Lemieux

8.9 Which defenseman holds the record for most goals in one season?

A. Bobby Orr
B. Doug Wilson
C. Paul Coffey
D. Denis Potvin

8.10 Name the only teenager besides Wayne Gretzky to register a 50-goal season.

A. Pierre Larouche
B. Mario Lemieux
C. Jimmy Carson
D. Dale Hawerchuk

8.11 Which individual award has Mike Bossy won most often?

A. The Art Ross (leading scorer)
B. The Lady Byng (sportsmanship)
C. The Conn Smythe (playoff MVP)
D. The Hart (League MVP)

8.12 Who scored the fastest hat trick?

A. Pete Mahovlich
B. Glenn Anderson
C. Bill Mosienko
D. Jean Beliveau

8.13 Next to Maurice and Henri Richard, which brothers are the most successful combined point-getters?

A. Bobby and Dennis Hull
B. Max and Doug Bentley
C. Gordie and Vic Howe
D. Frank and Pete Mahovlich

THE ICEMEN COMETH
Answers

8.1 A. He was ineligible because he'd been a WHA pro.

Gretzky has won almost every NHL award available to a forward, but like many of hockey's greatest (including Richard, Howe and Lafleur), he was denied the Calder — but for a different reason. Gretzky's season with the WHA's Edmonton Oilers put an end to his rookie status: the League considered his WHA experience a pro year. In that case, why don't his WHA points count in his career totals?

8.2 D. Darryl Sittler.

Sittler smashed the single-game record on February 7, 1976, scoring 10 points on six goals and four assists in an 11–4 Toronto romp over Boston. It was that kind of night: whenever the Leafs' captain was on the ice, something happened, including a goal he scored from behind the net! Needless to say, Sittler owned the Bruins — and goalie Dave Reece, who never played another NHL game.

8.3 B. Bobby Orr.

Orr became hockey's first millionaire after signing a multi-year contract with the Bruins in 1971. Shortly thereafter, in June 1972, the WHA's Winnipeg Jets inked Bobby Hull to a 10-year deal worth $2.75 million.

8.4 A. The player with the most goals.

Despite the tie for total points, Dionne won, based on the fact that he'd scored more goals. In his autobiography, *Gretzky*, Wayne asks: "What did that say to all the kids who'd heard a thousand times, 'an assist is as important as a goal'?"

8.5 B. Brad Park.

One of the League's most skilful offensive defensemen, Park was the perennial Norris runner-up during the 1970s, finishing behind Bobby Orr four times and being bested twice by Denis Potvin.

8.6 B. Peter Stastny.

Unequalled by anyone except Gretzky, Stastny scored 1,059 points in the 1980s. As a Nordique, Stastny became one of the League's most consistent point producers, recording +100 points in each of his first six seasons, a distinction he shares with only two other players, Gretzky and Mario Lemieux.

8.7 A. John Bucyk.

Less spectacular than Bruin teammates Orr and Esposito, Bucyk set his own record in 1971 by posting a +50-goal season at the age of 35.1. After labouring through some of Boston's best and worst years, Bucyk finally reached the 50-goal plateau in his 16th NHL season. Next oldest is Mullen (32.1), followed by Hadfield (31.6) and MacDonald (30.0).

8.8 D. Mario Lemieux.

In an 8–6 victory over New Jersey on December 31, 1988, Lemieux scored five goals in five different ways: even strength, power play, short-handed, penalty shot and empty-net goal. It was an NHL first.

8.9 C. Paul Coffey.

Coffey's 48-goal season in 1985–86 ended Orr's 11-year reign as top defensive goal-scorer. Orr set his 46-goal record in 1974–75.

8.10 C. Jimmy Carson.

Among the hot young snipers who've made their first NHL marks early in their careers, only Carson has equalled Gretzky by turning in a 50-goal season before his 20th birthday. Gretzky was 19.2 when he first passed the 50-goal mark; Carson, at 19.7, was only five months older when he netted +50 goals in his second NHL season, 1987–88. Next youngest were Larouche (20.5), Hawerchuk (21.1) and Lemieux (21.5).

8.11 B. The Lady Byng (sportsmanship).

Despite numerous NHL game and season records, four Stanley Cups and nine consecutive 50-goal seasons, Bossy never won a scoring title or League MVP honours. The Islanders' star *did* pick up one Conn Smythe (1982) and three Lady Byngs (1983/84/86).

8.12 C. Bill Mosienko.

Although Wayne Gretzky has scored the most hat tricks (+35), Chicago's Mosienko holds the record for fastest three goals. He pulverized the Rangers' Lorne Anderson at 6:09, 6:20 and 6:30 of the third period on March 23, 1952. Not a bad night's work: three goals in 21 seconds flat. Unlike Beliveau's 44-second hat trick in 1955, Mosienko's occurred while both teams were at full strength.

8.13 D. Frank and Pete Mahovlich.

Although plenty of brother duos have played in the NHL, few have racked up more than 1,000 career points combined. Sometimes one brother is exceptional (Gordie Howe, with 1,850 total points) whereas the other remains ordinary (Vic Howe, 7 total points), but most often it's a shared effort. Brothers Frank and Pete have 1,876 total points combined, the Howes 1,857, the Hulls 1,824 and the Bentleys 1,087. The Richards lead all brothers, with 2,011 points, but closing in fast are Marcel Dionne (1,771) and brother Gilbert (+34), who should surpass the Richards by 1995.

ROOTS: FATHERS, SONS & BROTHERS

"Brothers together play better" is an old hockey axiom proven true by sibling teammates like the Bentleys and the Stastnys — leading point-getters in the 1940s and 1980s, respectively. But brothers more often play on different lines (the Richards), different teams (the Courtnalls) or different positions (the Espositos). Some sons have made a name for themselves long after their famous fathers have hung up the blades.

Match the hockey families with their player positions.

(Answers are at the back of the book.)

Phil Esposito & Tony Esposito
Bert Lindsay & Ted Lindsay
Bryan Hextall, Jr., & Ron Hextall
Brian Murray & Terry Murray
Geoff Courtnall & Russ Courtnall
Sam LoPresti & Pete LoPresti
Gordie Howe & Mark Howe
Lionel Conacher & Brian Conacher
Ken Dryden & Dave Dryden
Barclay Plager & Bob Plager
Bobby Hull & Brett Hull
Murray Wilson & Doug Wilson

1._____ & _____
      Brother   Brother
  (Canadiens Goalie)   (Sabres Goalie)

2._____ & _____
      Father   Son
(Americans Defenseman)   (Maple Leafs Forward)

(Continues on page 80)

3._____ & _____

Father   Son
(Blackhawks Forward)   (Blues Forward)

4._____ & _____

Father   Son
(Blackhawks Goalie)   (North Stars Goalie)

5._____ & _____

Brother   Brother
(Red Wings Coach)   (Capitals Coach)

6._____ & _____

Father   Son
(Rangers Forward)   (Nordiques Goalie)

7._____ & _____

Brother   Brother
(Blues Defenseman)   (Blues Defenseman)

8._____ & _____

Father   Son
(Red Wings Forward)   (Flyers Defenseman)

9._____ & _____

Brother   Brother
(Bruins Forward)   (Chicago Goalie)

10._____ & _____

Father   Son
(Wanderers Goalie)   (Red Wings Forward)

11._____ & _____

Brother   Brother
(Canadiens Forward)   (Sharks Defenseman)

12._____ & _____

Brother   Brother
(North Stars Forward)   (Canucks Forward)

DROPPING THE GLOVES

There's no denying that fighting has given the game a black eye. But all players admit that sooner or later everyone is called to the dance. What is the "Piestany Punch-up"? Who is the all-time bad boy of hockey? In this quiz we pull no punches, offering a few fighting words to get a rise out of even the most apathetic fan. Watch out for the sucker-punch.

(Answers are at the end of the chapter.)

9.1 Who said: "Even if I wanted to go straight, I said to myself, I couldn't: there are too many enforcers around the league looking to take me on and prove they are number one"?

A. Dave Schultz
B. Bob Probert
C. Paul Holmgren
D. Dave Williams

9.2 Which teams were involved in the brawl that brought about the NHL's first All-Star game?

A. Blackhawks–Red Wings
B. Bruins–Maple Leafs
C. Senators–Rangers
D. Canadiens–Maroons

9.3 Name the only two 50-goal scorers in NHL history who, at some point in their careers, also led the League in penalty minutes.

A. Gary Roberts
B. Vic Hadfield
C. Maurice Richard
D. Rick Middleton

9.4 What two teams brawled on the ice *before* the start of a 1987 playoff game?

A. Red Wings–Blackhawks
B. Flyers–Canadiens
C. Jets–Flames
D. Islanders–Capitals

9.5 Who holds the record for most penalties in one game?

A. Dave Schultz
B. Jim Dorey
C. Chris Nilan
D. Terry O'Reilly

9.6 Which player received the longest NHL suspension ever for a playing infraction?

A. Dave Williams
B. Tom Lysiak
C. Shayne Corson
D. Bob Probert

9.7 A bomb exploded during a Detroit–Montreal game at the Forum in 1955, sparking the famous Maurice Richard riot. Where was the Rocket?

A. In the penalty box
B. In the Habs dressing room
C. In the stands
D. In the press box

9.8 Who is the NHL's all-time penalty leader?

A. Chris Nilan
B. Dave Schultz
C. Dave Williams
D. Dale Hunter

9.9 Which 1991–92 50-goal scorer received the most penalty minutes?

A. Jeremy Roenick
B. Kevin Stevens
C. Brett Hull
D. Gary Roberts

9.10 What is the "Piestany Punch-up"?

A. The 1972 Canada Cup fracas
B. A nickname for a Czech referee
C. A World Junior Championship brawl
D. A Soviet enforcer tactic

DROPPING THE GLOVES
Answers

9.1 A. Dave Schultz.

They didn't call him "The Hammer" for nothing. In the 1970s Schultz was the baddest Broad Street Bully, racking up misconducts and fighting majors faster than you can say, "Philadelphia, City of Brotherly Love." He did have one 20-goal season, but Schultz was the game's chief goon, defending his title every game. Between 1972 and 1975, Schultz accounted for 22 percent of all penalty minutes amassed by the Flyers, the most penalized team in hockey. His 1974–75 record for most penalty minutes (472) in one season remains unbeaten.

9.2 B. Bruins–Maple Leafs.

The NHL's first All-Star game was a benefit match for Toronto's Ace Bailey, who had been seriously injured in a Bruins–Maple Leafs fight in 1934. Boston's Eddie Shore, retaliating for a trip by King Clancy, mistook Bailey for Clancy and charged him from behind. Bailey struck the ice, fracturing his skull; he lay twisted and twitching in a seizure-like state. The Leafs' Red Horner then decked Shore, knocking him cold on the ice. Both teams stormed over the boards. The mêlée ended with Horner and Conacher holding off the Bruins with sticks raised bayonet-fashion. Near death for 10 days, Bailey recovered and was well enough to attend his benefit All-Star game and shake hands with Shore at centre ice. For the rest of the season, the Bruins wore helmets. Bailey never played another game.

9.3 B. Vic Hadfield and C. Maurice Richard.

No NHLer has ever managed to score 50 goals and become penalty leader in the same season, but Hadfield and Richard earn a footnote in history as the only players who did both in a career. Hadfield served a League-leading 151 minutes in the box (1963–64) and, eight years later (in 1971–72), scored 50 goals to become the only Ranger ever to post a 50-goal season. Surprisingly, Richard, the NHL's first 50-goal scorer (in 1944–45's 50-game schedule) was no slouch when it came to box time, more than doubling his career record (544 goals) with 1285 career penalty minutes. But Richard's fame has never been measured in penalties, and when, in 1952–53, he amassed a League-leading 112 minutes, it beat Terrible Ted Lindsay's season mark by only one minute!

9.4 B. Flyers–Canadiens.

During the Wales Conference finals, a bizarre pre-game brawl erupted at the end of the warm-up period when two Flyers tried to prevent the Canadiens from performing their pre-game ritual of shooting the puck into Philly's empty net. As most players were heading to the dressing rooms, Flyers goalie Chico Resch streaked back onto the ice and threw his stick at the puck while hitman Ed Hospodar took on Montreal's Shayne Corson and Claude Lemieux. Within seconds, both teams were engaged in a full-scale battle. Officials handed out $24,000 in fines.

9.5 C. Chris Nilan.

It wasn't a good night for hockey on March 31, 1991, when Hartford met Boston in a $3\frac{1}{2}$-hour free-for-all that saw 10 misconducts handed out. Nilan's pugilistic skills made him the busiest man on the ice that night, collecting 42 penalty minutes in a record 10 penalties, including six minors, two majors, one 10-minute misconduct and one game misconduct.

9.6 B. Tom Lysiak.

After being thrown out of the faceoff circle by linesman Ron Foyt in 1982, Chicago's Lysiak waited till the puck was dropped, skated to the Blackhawk bench where Foyt was standing, and deliberately took the feet out from under him. At his disciplinary hearing, Lysiak was suspended for 20 games for physical abuse of an official.

9.7 C. In the stands.

Richard was sitting directly behind the Detroit goal, about 40 feet away from Clarence Campbell. The NHL president had suspended Richard earlier that week for deliberately punching an official during a game. The suspension included the season's final three games and the playoffs. At stake were Richard's scoring lead, the Canadiens' first-place finish and the Stanley Cup. For Montreal fans, losing Richard — their idol and Montreal's best player — was a slap in the face. Ironically, the tear gas bomb, obviously targeted for Campbell, exploded very close to Richard's seat. The game was cancelled and rioting spilled out onto Montreal streets. Only a radio appeal by Richard quieted the city. All was lost: the Rocket's scoring title, the Habs' first-place finish and the Cup finals. To this day, Jean Beliveau believes that with Richard's help the Canadiens would have won the Stanley Cup in 1955.

9.8 C. Dave Williams.

Over 13 seasons, Williams averaged 4.12 minutes per game in the box. With his total of 3,966 penalty minutes, Williams accumulated almost 1,000 minutes more than his nearest rival. Altogether Williams has spent about 74 games, or one entire season, penalized!

9.9 B. Kevin Stevens.

You've got to be playing your career best when you finish second overall in League scoring with 123 points — only 9 back of Mario Lemieux — and yet still spend as much time in the box as heavyweight Chris Nilan. Despite his 252 penalty minutes, Stevens scored 54 goals in 1991–92, more than Roberts (219 PIM/53 goals), Roenick (98 PIM/53 goals) and Hull (48 PIM/70 goals).

9.10 C. A World Junior Championship brawl.

It was the most violent mêlée in the history of international hockey. The Soviets, out of medal contention, had nothing to lose. Team Canada was applying the pressure, trying to increase a 4–2 lead and go for the gold medal. Then it happened. Canadian and Soviet players, fed up with stickwork and running at each other, dropped their gloves and engaged in a 20-minute brawl that cleared the benches. With the fight out of control, the officials left the ice and the arena lights dimmed. The game never resumed. Both teams were disqualified, and their records were erased.

CROSSWORD #3

FAMOUS NICKNAMES

(Answers to crosswords are at the back of the book.)

Across

1 Flyer's Moose
4. Glen Sather
9. Goalie Frank Brimsek, "Mr._____"
10. "Golden _____"
11. Rogatien Vachon
12. "Cyclone" _____
15. Mario Lemieux
17. Derek Sanderson
19. "Black Jack" _____
22. Million dollar _____
24. Leaf/Hab coach, init. (2 ltrs.)
25. "_____" Joe Malone
26. Ex-Oiler/Ranger centre
30. Harold Ballard (2 wrds.)
32. Tim Horton
33. The "uncheckable" Czech
34. Ex-Leaf coach: "Grey Eagle"
36. _____ Anderson
38. "____ Poison" Stewart
39. Sergio Momesso
40. "Chico" _____
43. "____ Goalie," abbrv.
46. "_____" Ted Lindsay
48. "Mr. Elbows"
50. Lester Patrick, "_____ Fox"
51. Ex-Flyer, 50-goal man
52. Chris Nilan

Down

1. Bobby Schmautz, "___ Hook," abbrv.
2. Cecil "Babe" _____
3. "_____" Lalonde (5 ltrs.)
4. "The Edmonton Express," Eddie _____
5. Isles coach, 1st name
6. Howie Morenz, "Stratford _____"
7. "Chicoutimi Cucumber," 1st name, clue: goalie trophy
8. Hector Blake
10. "_____ the Snake" Plante
13. Nike _____
14. Forward position, init.
16. Espo
17. Kind of goal, "____-in"
18. Yvan Cournoyer
20. Old pro league, init. (3 ltrs.)
21. Kind of penalty
23. Harry "Apple Cheeks" _____
27. Don Cherry
28. Flyer "Chief," init.
29. Dave Williams
31. Clarence "____" Day
32. Frank Mahovlich
34. "Bad Joe" Hall, init. (3 ltrs.)
35. Dave Schultz
37. "_____ defenseman back"
41. Alan Eagleson
42. Mike Keenan: "Dr._____"
44. "Ole Bootnose," Wings coach
45. Mark Messier
46. Esa Tikkanen
47. Leonard Kelly
49. Harry "Pee-____" Oliver

"TWO FOR THE SHOW"

The game, after all, is a show, and not only a show of hockey skills: it's entertainment. Players become stars, celebrities on ice. They are scrutinized and idolized on trading cards, the sports pages and TV highlight features. This quiz spotlights your knowledge of hockey's influence beyond the game on the ice. Tickets, please.

(Answers are at the end of the chapter.)

10.1 Where and when was NHL hockey first broadcast on a pay-per-view basis?

    A. In New York for the 1979 Challenge Cup

    B. In Long Island for the 1983 All-Star game

    C. In Minnesota for the 1991 Stanley Cup

    D. In Chicago for the 1992 Stanley Cup

10.2 What are actor Paul Newman's hockey name and number in the movie *Slapshot*?

    A. Butch Cassidy, No .9

    B. Jimmy Lindsay, No. 12

    C. Reggie Dunlop, No. 7

    D. Gus Morton, No. 6

10.3 In the TV sitcom "Cheers," how does Carla's husband, goalie Eddie Lebec, die?

A. At the hands of Carla, who goes temporarily insane after finding out Eddie cheated on her

B. In a freak Zamboni accident at an ice show

C. In an on-ice brawl at Boston Garden

D. He's electrocuted at Sam's bar while installing a jukebox.

10.4 What is the most valuable hockey trading card?

A. Bobby Orr's rookie card, 1966–67 (Tops)

B. Howie Morenz, 1934 (O-Pee-Chee)

C. Bobby Hull's rookie card, 1957–58 (Tops)

D. Gordie Howe's rookie card, 1951–52 (Parkhurst)

10.5 TV cameras have shot the game from every angle. But who first wore a camera *on* the ice during an NHL pre-season game?

A. It's never been done.

B. Defenseman Larry Robinson

C. Goalie Kelly Hrudey

D. Referee Don Kohorski

10.6 What ever happened to Foster Hewitt's famous broadcast booth, the gondola?

A. It's stored in Maple Leaf Gardens.

B. It was trashed.

C. The Hewitt family has it.

D. It's on display in the Hockey Hall of Fame.

10.7 Gump Worsley opened a Montreal restaurant that featured "The Ranger Special" on the menu. What was "The Ranger Special"?

A. Pigs' knuckles

B. New York cheesecake

C. Stuffed eggs

D. Chicken salad

10.8 What was "The Great Canadian"?

    A. An advertising slogan for Canadian beer
    B. A Winnipeg radio program
    C. An American nickname for Eddie Shore
    D. An unproduced Hollywood hockey movie

10.9 Which team accounted for the highest percentage of all NHL merchandise sold in 1991–92?

    A. The New York Rangers
    B. The San Jose Sharks
    C. The Los Angeles Kings
    D. The Chicago Blackhawks

10.10 What company did Wayne Gretzky and Vladislav Tretiak endorse together on television?

    A. Coca-Cola
    B. American Express
    C. Gillette
    D. Pro Set Table-Top Hockey

10.11 Who said: "I went to a fight and a hockey game broke out"?

    A. Eddie Shack
    B. Jay Leno
    C. Henny Youngman
    D. Rodney Dangerfield

10.12 What inspired hockey's three-star selection?

    A. The name of a sponsor's product
    B. A Gordie Howe hat trick in 1948
    C. Dwindling attendance during the third period
    D. A newspaper's promotional gimmick

10.13 How many hockey players have appeared on the cover of *Time* magazine?

A. 1
B. 4
C. 7
D. 10

10.14 What hockey broadcaster first coined the phrase "dipsy-doodler"?

A. Danny Gallivan
B. Dan Kelly
C. Foster Hewitt
D. Dick Irvin

10.15 What's the Bull Ring?

A. A boxing/sports gym in Boston
B. An ex-gambling hangout in Maple Leaf Gardens
C. A hockey tavern near the Montreal Forum
D. The organ balcony in Chicago Stadium

10.16 The majority of NHL clubs make the most money from:

A. Television
B. Skyboxes
C. Ticket sales
D. Concessions

"TWO FOR THE SHOW"
Answers

10.1 C. In Minnesota for the 1991 Stanley Cup.

Hockey's introduction to pay-per-view TV received rave reviews and generated huge revenues spurred on by the North Stars' Cinderella performance in the 1991 playoffs.

Viewers were charged $9.95 per game in the first two rounds and $12.95 per game for the Conference and Cup finals. Minnesota's 11 home games attracted 300,000 viewers and brought in $3.5 million.

10.2 C. Reggie Dunlop, No. 7.

Newman portrays player-coach Dunlop of the fictitious Charlestown Chiefs, a failing hockey team whose fortunes turn around after it acquires the Hansens, three brothers in horn-rimmed glasses who are better at cracking skulls than playing hockey. In classic Hollywood fashion, the Chiefs start winning games and the hometown crowds return to cheer on their misguided heroes.

10.3 B. In a freak Zamboni accident at an ice show.

The producers of "Cheers" kill off the Lebec character — who's joined a travelling ice show as a skating penguin — in an episode where Eddie dies while saving a fellow penguin from a berserk Zamboni. Bonus Question: What's Carla and Eddie's special song? "O, Canada," of course.

10.4 D. Gordie Howe's rookie card, 1951–52 (Parkhurst).

In contrast to the astronomical prices baseball cards command, hockey's most valuable card is a rookie Howe, listed at $2,500 and worth $4,000 in mint condition. (The first card issued of a player is called his "rookie card," even when, as in Howe's case, the card is issued after the player's rookie season.) In mint shape, Orr will bring $3,000, Hull $2,200 and Morenz $1,000.

10.5 C. Goalie Kelly Hrudey.

In a 1991 Rangers–Kings exhibition game at Caesar's Palace in Las Vegas, Hrudey's helmet was wired with a micro-camera, permitting viewers to experience hockey from the player's perspective for the first time.

10.6 B. It was trashed.

Two generations of Canadians grew up (as did the game itself) listening to Foster Hewitt call the play-by-play from the gondola in Maple Leaf Gardens. In 1979, the famous announcers' booth was torn down to make way for private boxes.

10.7 D. Chicken salad.

The Gumper had a great sense of humour, especially about his teammates. With Ranger backchecking often non-existent, his years in the New York nets were packed with 50-shot games. But Worsley took the puck barrage in stride and tossed the last laugh: chicken salad, "The Ranger Special."

10.8 D. An unproduced Hollywood hockey movie.

While the L.A. Kings play the lead role in attracting celebrities to hockey today, in the thirties and forties the big draw was Broadway's Blueshirts. New York's show-biz crowd loved the Rangers, who became the hottest ticket in the Big Apple. On hockey night Madison Square Garden was *the* place to be, drawing sports personalities and entertainers like Lucille Ball, Humphrey Bogart and Cab Calloway. Little wonder that a few Rangers were cast in "The Great Canadian," an MGM production starring Clark Gable as a dashing hockey hero and Myrna Loy as the love interest. Alas, the film was nixed in pre-production.

10.9 B. The San Jose Sharks.

They may have finished in the cellar, but the Sharks manhandled — by far — all other NHL clubs in merchandising, accounting for 27 percent of League sales, or about U.S. $35 million gross. That's big money, ranking the Sharks second only to the Chicago Bulls in all American sports merchandising.

10.10 C. Gillette.

The Gretzky–Tretiak commercial for Gillette — the first North American TV ad to use a Soviet athlete — featured a nose-to-nose match-up between two of hockey's greatest, playing . . . table-top hockey.

10.11 D. Rodney Dangerfield.

A favourite on the comedy circuit, Mr. Respectability first cracked hockey's best one-liner on "The Tonight Show Starring Johnny Carson" in 1983.

10.12 A. The name of a sponsor's product.

The three-star selection originated in 1936 on "The Hot Stove League," a radio program broadcast across North America and sponsored by Imperial Oil, which advertised "Imperial 3 Star" gasoline. Old-time greats like Syl Apps and Joe Primeau originally chose the three stars.

10.13 C. 7.

Sports figures have rarely commanded enough attention to be featured in a *Time* cover story. Since 1923, it has happened seven times — and, amazingly, not to Howe, Orr or Richard. Wayne Gretzky has graced *Time*'s cover (March 1985), although The Great One had to share it with basketball superstar Larry Bird. Flyers goalie Bernie Parent also made *Time* (February 1975), as did the Canada–Russia series (October 1974), Phil Esposito (October 1972), Bobby Hull (March 1968), Davey Kerr (March 1938) and Lorne Chabot (February 1935).

10.14 C. Foster Hewitt.

"Dipsy-doodler" isn't in any dictionary, but it's long been in hockey's lexicon, thanks to Foster Hewitt and later Danny Gallivan. In the 1940s, Hewitt called Maple Leafs superstar Max Bentley a "dipsy-doodler" to describe the forward's slight build and adroit skating and stick-handling skills. Gallivan, a wordsmith in his own right, made "dipsy-doodler" a hockey standard in the 1960s.

10.15 B. An ex-gambling hangout in Maple Leaf Gardens.

In 1946, Toronto boss Conn Smythe cleaned out the gamblers and bookies who hung out in the section of the Gardens' concourse known as the "Bull Ring."

10.16 C. Ticket sales.

The NHL's richest teams make about $400,000 per game; average ticket prices range from $18 in Washington to $30 in New York. Receipts from television, skyboxes and concession are significantly lower.

THE WRITE STUFF

For this quiz, it doesn't matter how many hockey books you've read. Knowing something or anything about the players on the left will help you match them up with their books on the right. And don't look for *Hockey: Here's Howe, Robinson for the Defence* or *Fuhr on Goaltending*. That's like a breakaway on an empty net!

(Answers are at the back of the book.)

Part 1

1. ____ Don Cherry
2. ____ Dave Schultz
3. ____ Ken Dryden
4. ____ Brad Park
5. ____ Vern Buffey
6. ____ Dick Irvin
7. ____ Vladislav Tretiak

a. *The Art of Goaltending*
b. *Play the Man*
c. *The Habs*
d. *Grapes*
e. *The Game*
f. *The Hammer*
g. *Black, White & Never Right*

Part 2

1. ____ Derek Sanderson
2. ____ John Ferguson
3. ____ Guy Lafleur
4. ____ Punch Imlach
5. ____ Eric Lindros
6. ____ Foster Hewitt
7. ____ Colleen & Gordie Howe

a. *Fire on Ice*
b. *Hockey Night in Canada*
c. *After the Applause*
d. *Hockey Is a Battle*
e. *Overtime*
f. *I've Got to Be Me*
g. *Thunder & Lightning*

ALL FOR ONE

Team character. You don't win championships without that special melding of leadership, talent and brawn. It's a force born of a collective desire to win, to be the best. Along the way, a team develops a personality and a history as interesting as those of the stars themselves. In this quiz we focus only on hockey teams and their stories.

(Answers are at the end of the chapter.)

11.1 Which currently active hockey club took the fewest years after being founded to win the Cup?

    A. The Montreal Canadiens
    B. The Edmonton Oilers
    C. The New York Rangers
    D. The Ottawa Senators

11.2 What was the main difference between the Montreal Canadiens and the Montreal Maroons?

    A. The Maroons never once played in the Montreal Forum.
    B. The Maroons were English and the Canadiens were French.
    C. The Maroons and Canadiens played in different pro leagues.
    D. The Maroons never won the Stanley Cup.

11.3 What caused the city of Hamilton, Ontario, to lose its NHL franchise in 1925?

A. Financial difficulties
B. A political scandal
C. A players' labour dispute
D. A power struggle over Toronto's territorial rights

11.4 Which NHL team had the rights to Gordie Howe but rejected him in 1943?

A. The New York Rangers
B. The Detroit Red Wings
C. The Toronto Maple Leafs
D. The Chicago Blackhawks

11.5 According to Chicago's original charter, what is the club's real name?

A. The Hawks
B. The Blackhawks
C. The Black Hawks
D. The Black-Eyed Hawks

11.6 Name the first American-based team to win the Stanley Cup.

A. The St. Louis Eagles
B. The Seattle Metropolitans
C. The New York Rangers
D. The Brooklyn Americans

11.7 Name the first pro hockey team in Pittsburgh.

A. The Pittsburgh Hornets
B. The Pittsburgh Penguins
C. The Pittsburgh Pirates
D. The Pittsburgh Yellow Jackets

11.8 Name the NHL team that won the Stanley Cup with the worst regular-season record.

A. The 1949 Maple Leafs
B. The 1925 Victoria Cougars
C. The 1938 Chicago Blackhawks
D. The 1929 Boston Bruins

11.9 Which NHL team sported the oldest line-up ever to win the Stanley Cup?

A. The 1927 Ottawa Senators
B. The 1943 Detroit Red Wings
C. The 1967 Toronto Maple Leafs
D. The 1969 Montreal Canadiens

11.10 Which NHL team caused the League to adopt the co-incidental minor rule requiring teams penalized at the same time to substitute players so five skaters remain on each side?

A. The Hartford Whalers
B. The New York Islanders
C. The Philadelphia Flyers
D. The Edmonton Oilers

ALL FOR ONE
Answers

11.1 C. The New York Rangers.

Of the 12 current NHL teams that have won the Stanley Cup, only the Rangers, organized in 1926, recorded their first championship in their second season of operation, 1927–28. Under manager-coach Lester Patrick, the underdog Rangers won a wild best-of-five series that featured one of hockey's most memorable moments. In Game Two, with no goalie available to replace an injured Lorne

Chabot, the 44-year-old Patrick strapped on the pads himself and skated to instant fame, backstopping the Rangers to victory in sudden-death overtime. Perhaps inspired by the heroics of their ageless leader, New York won the Stanley Cup right on Forum ice, defeating the Maroons in a Game Five thriller.

11.2 B. The Maroons were English and the Canadiens were French.

As rivalries go, few are as intense as that created by the French–English fact in Montreal. From the start, the Canadiens were a team of French-speaking players, organized to draw interest from Montreal's francophone population. The Maroons joined the NHL only with the approval of the Canadiens, who sold half their territorial rights to the English team, an act more business-wise than generous. The Maroons–Canadiens rivalry in the 1920s and 1930s worked as planned, capitalizing on Montreal's love of hockey and its proudly bilingual nature. The Maroons won two Stanley Cups before folding in 1938.

11.3 C. A players' labour dispute.

In their brief five-season history, the Hamilton Tigers' best shot at an NHL championship came in 1925. After finishing first, Hamilton team members refused to play postseason unless financially compensated for the playoffs. It was the NHL's first labour dispute, and president Frank Calder settled it by calling the striking players' bluff. The Tigers stood firm on their demands; they were suspended — losing any chance of winning a Stanley Cup; and the Hamilton franchise moved to New York the following season.

11.4 A. The New York Rangers.

At a 1943 training camp in Winnipeg, New York managers weren't impressed enough to sign the shy, awkward 15-year-old from Floral, Saskatchewan. Howe went home dejected but tried out the next year at a Red Wings camp. In one play, the big kid split the defense, shifted his stick to the left side and potted a goal. The play raised a few eyebrows, including those of Detroit GM Jack Adams, who wasted no time in inking Howe to his first pro contract.

11.5 B. The Blackhawks.

Until 1986, the team's name had always been written as two words. That year, club owner Bill Wirtz officially changed the spelling to conform to Chicago's original NHL charter of 1926. The name was mis-written on everything from League scoresheets to club publicity for 60 years.

11.6 B. The Seattle Metropolitans.

When the Metros defeated the Canadiens in 1916–17, Seattle became the first American city to claim the Cup. In those days, the Stanley Cup was a challenge trophy, disputed by pro teams from the eastern and western leagues. The first American-based NHL team to win the Cup, the New York Rangers, did so in 1927–28.

11.7 A. The Pittsburgh Hornets.

Steel Town has a great hockey history, and it began long before Mario Lemieux or the 1967 NHL expansion. In fact, 15 years before the NHL started, in an era of amateur hockey, Pittsburgh was playing the game and paying its players an unprecedented $30 a week. And they skated on artificial ice — 10 years before Canada got its first artificial rink. The Penguins are today's heroes, but the fans first started cheering in Pittsburgh many years ago for teams like the Hornets, the Pirates and the Yellow Jackets.

11.8 C. The 1938 Chicago Blackhawks.

When the 1990–91 North Stars finished their season 27–39–14, few expected them to reach the semi-, Conference, or Cup finals. In fact, they became only the 15th team in

NHL history with a regular-season record below .500 to make it to the finals. Like most of those other 14 contenders, Minnesota lost, but two of the teams did win the Cup: the '49 Maple Leafs (22–25–13) and the '38 Blackhawks, who posted a miserable 14–25–9, or a .385 average. How did they go so far on so little? The Hawks first edged out the Canadiens and Americans, two teams whose own averages were barely above .500. In the finals, the Maple Leafs were another matter. But the Hawks were on a roll. Substitute goaltending won their first game; a disputed goal took another; and the best-of-five series was decided in Chicago as the Hawks coasted to Cup victory before a hysterical home crowd. It was pure heart that brought Chicago the Cup in 1938. The next season, they finished in the cellar.

11.9 C. The 1967 Toronto Maple Leafs.

With an average age of 31, Punch Imlach's 1967 Leafs iced the oldest Stanley Cup champions. Built around veterans like George Armstrong, Marcel Pronovost and Tim Horton, all of whom were 37, the aging Leafs even included three seniors over 40: Johnny Bower, Allan Stanley and Red Kelly. Toronto took the Cup in six games from highly favoured Montreal, a team whose own average age was 28.

11.10 D. The Edmonton Oilers.

In the early 1980s, the NHL adopted the "Edmonton Oilers" rule, so named because the Oilers often purposely drew the opposition into coincidental minors. With both teams short-handed, the open ice gave Edmonton's speedy, finesse game an advantage that often resulted in an Oilers goal. The rule all but eliminated hockey's four-on-four situation until 1992–93, when the NHL decided to return to no substitutions for coincidental minors.

"HOW 'BOUT THEM TIGERS!"

Pirates. Eagles. Tigers. Names more evocative of American sports than of hockey. But teams like the Eagles played the game and challenged for the Stanley Cup long before the Bruins, Rangers or Blackhawks. Franchises existed in Seattle, Quebec and Ottawa — all Stanley Cup winners!

Match these present-day NHL cities with their original hockey teams.

(Answers are at the back of the book.)

Part 1

1. _____ Edmonton	a.	Victorias
2. _____ St. Louis	b.	Senators
3. _____ New York	c.	Eskimos
4. _____ Winnipeg	d.	Quakers
5. _____ Philadelphia	e.	Americans
6. _____ Ottawa	f.	Eagles

Part 2

1. _____ Pittsburgh	a.	Millionaires
2. _____ Toronto	b.	Bulldogs
3. _____ Quebec	c.	Pirates
4. _____ Detroit	d.	Falcons
5. _____ Vancouver	e.	St. Pats
6. _____ Calgary	f.	Maroons
7. _____ Montreal	g.	Tigers

CHAPTER 12

IN SEARCH OF SILVER

No matter how many goals you score or records you break, in hockey you're not a winner till you bring home the Stanley Cup. It's what every kid dreams of and every player strives towards. Each spring the year's best are rewarded with hockey's greatest honour.

(Answers are at the end of the chapter.)

12.1 Any player who's sipped champagne from the Stanley Cup knows the inscription on the inside of the Cup's bowl. What is it?

A. "Congratulations, Chaps"

B. "Lord Stanley of Preston, Queen's Representative, Dominion of Canada"

C. Stanley's favourite Tennyson poem, "The Charge of the Light Brigade"

D. The names of the Stanley Cup champions of 1907

12.2 Bob Johnson was only the third American ever to coach a Stanley Cup championship team. Who were the first two American coaches?

A. The Canadiens' Leo Dandurand

B. The Flyers' Fred Shero

C. The Islanders' Al Arbour

D. The Blackhawks' Bill Stewart

12.3 The Rangers won their last Stanley Cup on an overtime goal in Game Six against Toronto in 1940. Who scored that Cup-winning goal?

A. The father of Penguins GM Craig Patrick
B. The grandfather of goalie Ron Hextall
C. The father of broadcaster Dick Irvin
D. The grandfather of winger Tim Kerr

12.4 How many women's names are engraved on the Stanley Cup?

A. None
B. 1
C. 2
D. 3

12.5 What team made the greatest comeback in Stanley Cup history?

A. The 1942 Maple Leafs
B. The 1967 Maple Leafs
C. The 1971 Montreal Canadiens
D. The 1975 New York Islanders

12.6 What were the Las Vegas odds on Minnesota winning the Stanley Cup in 1991?

A. 10 to 1
B. 15 to 1
C. 20 to 1
D. 25 to 1

12.7 Who called Canadiens coach Al MacNeil "incompetent" and "the worst coach I ever played for" during the 1971 Stanley Cup finals?

A. Pete Mahovlich
B. Henri Richard
C. John Ferguson
D. Rogatien Vachon

12.8 How many hats were thrown on the ice by Chicago fans after Dirk Graham scored his third goal in the last game of the 1992 Stanley Cup finals?

A. 111
B. 211
C. 311
D. 411

12.9 Who named his newborn son "Stanley" after winning the Cup?

A. Al Arbour
B. John Muckler
C. Scotty Bowman
D. Glen Sather

12.10 Only a few players have won the Stanley Cup with more than one team. What is the highest number of clubs with which one individual has won the Cup? (Name the player.)

A. 2
B. 3
C. 4
D. 5

12.11 In the 1950s, what team refused to shake hands with their opponents after losing the Stanley Cup finals?

A. The Detroit Red Wings
B. The New York Rangers
C. The Toronto Maple Leafs
D. The Montreal Canadiens

12.12 Which American team has won the Stanley Cup most often?

A. The Detroit Red Wings
B. The Boston Bruins
C. The New York Islanders
D. The Chicago Blackhawks

12.13 As one of the five original NHL charter-member teams, the Ottawa Senators were silver-rich in Stanley Cups. How many did the club win before folding in 1934?

A. 4
B. 6
C. 8
D. 10

12.14 How many miles did the Pittsburgh Penguins travel during the 1992 playoffs to win the Stanley Cup?

A. 4,656
B. 6,656
C. 12,656
D. 14,656

IN SEARCH OF SILVER
Answers

12.1 D. The names of the Stanley Cup champions of 1907.

Inside Lord Stanley's bowl is engraved: "Montreal Wanderers — Stanley Cup Champions 1906–07" and the line-up: "W. S. Strachan, Riley Hern, Lester Patrick, Hod Stuart, Frank Glass, Ernie Russell, Cecil Blachford, Ernie Johnson, Rod Kennedy, Jack Marshall, R. R. Boon."

12.2 A & D. The Canadiens' Leo Dandurand & The Black-hawks' Bill Stewart.

Massachusetts-born Stewart, a National League umpire, coached the Blackhawks to Cup victory in 1938; Dandurand, born in Illinois, owned and managed the Canadiens as well as coaching his "Flying Frenchmen" to three Cups (1924/30/31).

12.3 B. The grandfather of goalie Ron Hextall.

Three generations of Hextalls have played in the NHL: Ron's father, Bryan junior; his uncle, Dennis; and his grandfather, Bryan Hextall, Sr., who potted the Rangers' overtime Cup winner in the 1940 finals. Hextall senior was a superstar winger, a tough player with great speed and stick-handling skills, qualities he passed on to grandson Ron (whose own combative spirit and stickwork have earned him most penalty minutes and most goals — 2 — by a goalie). Hextall senior's linemate was Lynn Patrick, father of Craig Patrick; Dick Irvin, Sr.'s career as Maple Leafs coach ended after that 1940 overtime loss to the Rangers. And New York goalie Davey Kerr? No relation to ex-Flyer All-Star Tim Kerr.

12.4 D. 3.

Marguerite Norris, Sonia Scurfield and Marie Denise DeBartolo are the only women whose names appear on the Cup. Norris became the NHL's first female executive upon the death of her father, James Norris, serving as president of the Red Wings when Detroit won the Cup in 1954 and 1955. In 1989, Calgary Flames co-owner Scurfield became the second woman, and DeBartolo, ex-president of the Penguins, was added when Pittsburgh took the Cup in 1991.

12.5 A. The 1942 Maple Leafs.

Only one team in North American pro sports history has ever come back from a 0–3 deficit in a championship series.

After losing the first three games of the 1942 Stanley Cup finals to the underdog Red Wings, the Leafs began their astonishing turnaround, stealing a 4–3 victory in Detroit and outplaying the Wings in the next two contests to 9–3 and 3–0 wins. Game Seven produced Canada's largest hockey crowd of the era. The Gardens were jammed with 16,218 fans, who cheered the Leafs on to another come-from-behind win. Down one goal in the third period, Toronto scored three times, defeating Detroit and capturing the Maple Leafs' second Stanley Cup.

12.6 D. 25 to 1.

The North Stars of 1991 were one of hockey's great Cinderella teams. But any betting man who followed Minnesota's second half (14–6–6) might have given coach Bob Gainey better odds than 25 to 1, even though his club faced hockey's hottest team, Chicago, in Round One. The fairy tale almost came true — the Blackhawks went down in six, followed by St. Louis in six and Edmonton in five — but Minnesota ran out of stardust in Game Six against Bob Johnson's Penguins.

12.7 B. Henri Richard.

In Game Five of the Montreal–Chicago finals, frustration set in for Richard, who, after numerous line changes, complained openly about MacNeil's behind-the-bench tactics. Richard later regretted having made the comments, but he spoke volumes on the ice in Game Seven by scoring the final two goals in the 3–2 Cup-winning victory.

12.8 C. 311.

Tossing your hat on the ice after a Blackhawks hat trick is an old Chicago Stadium tradition. In that final Cup game, 311 hats hit the ice in honour of Hawks captain Graham, who had tied the game three times in the first period. So what happens to the hats? Another Chicago tradition dictates that they go to the player honoured: in this case, Dirk Graham.

12.9 C. Scotty Bowman.

A month after winning his first Cup with the Canadiens in 1973, Scotty named his first son Stanley Bowman.

12.10 C. 4.

Jack Marshall's 16-year career reads like a Who's Who of championship teams from hockey's youth. His name is engraved on the Stanley Cup five times, with four different teams — the 1901 Winnipeg Victorias, the 1902 Montreal AAA, the 1907 and 1910 Montreal Wanderers and the 1914 Toronto Blueshirts.

12.11 D. The Montreal Canadiens.

The 1954 Red Wings–Habs Cup finals are remembered as one of the closest and most exciting championship series ever played — and one of the most bitterly fought. Down three games to one, the Canadiens regrouped to tie the series and force a seventh game in Detroit. With the whole season at stake, the game went into overtime to decide a 1–1 deadlock. Four minutes later, Detroit's Tony Leswick cleared a pass into the Montreal zone, it deflected off Doug Harvey's glove, and the puck went right past shocked goalie Gerry McNeil. A cheap goal ended the Stanley Cup finals, and the Canadiens skated off before the customary handshakes.

12.12 A. The Detroit Red Wings.

Although the Red Wings haven't won the Cup since 1955 or been to the finals in decades, their seven championships have yet to be equalled by any other American team. The Bruins have five Cup victories, the Islanders four and the Blackhawks three.

12.13 D. 10.

The Senators were *the* powerhouse franchise in hockey's early years, winning 10 Cups, four of them in the NHL's first 10 seasons. In the pre-NHL era, when teams played seven to a side, the club was nicknamed the Silver Seven.

12.14 A. 4,656.

Considering that Cup finalists play best-of-seven series in four rounds, jetting between NHL buildings scattered across North America, it's amazing that the Penguins only travelled 4,656 miles to victory. Although the 1992 champs dispatched the Bruins and the Blackhawks in the minimum four games, geography played the biggest part in cutting down on their flyer miles. No league franchise is closer to more eastern and mid-western NHL cities than Pittsburgh.

PLAYOFF ACTION

(Answers to crosswords are at the back of the book.)

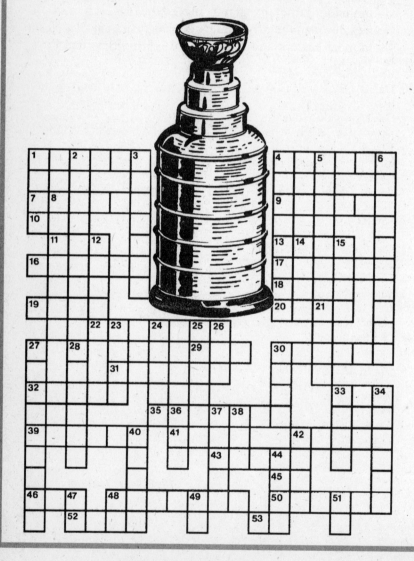

Across

1. _____ death
4. Coach with six Cups
7. 1974 Cup champs
9. _____-up
10. 1st name, Leaf capt. of 1948 Cup winner
11. Site of 1991 Cup victory, _____ Centre
13. Sid _____
16. Kevin _____
17. Ex-Flyer & Caps., Bob _____
18. Devils' Quebecker, init. (2 ltrs.)
19. Goalie, established most playoff wins in one season
20. 10 to 1 _____ against
22. Youngest Wing capt. ever
29. Calgary colour
30. Rangers' farm team in '30s
31. "Pocket _____"
32. "Super _____"
33. _____ Gilbert
35. Czech defector, '81 Rookie
39. Franchise _____, pl.
41. Lightning GM
42. Running out of _____
43. Ex-Flyer, most goals, one playoff year (1976)
45. "Perfect score"
46. Parry Sound native
48. 3-Cup-winning team is a _____
50. Toronto team before Leafs (2 wrds.)
52. Team with most Cups
53. Extra period, init.

Down

1. _____ shot
2. Goalie who won Playoff MVP before Rookie-of-the-Year (6 ltrs.)
3. Habs' 1st European
4. Goalie with 11 straight playoff wins in 1992
5. Score the game _____ (6 ltrs.)
6. 1991 Cup finalist finished below .500 in reg. season (2 wrds.)
8. Double Conn Smythe winner
12. 1st name, all-time shutout leader
14. _____-dogs, part-time scouts
15. A 3–2 _____ for Hartford
21. Fake fall
23. Shutout number
24. 1899 Cup winner, Mtl. Sham _____
25. 1918 Toronto Cup winners
26. Open _____
27. Donut franchise (2 wrds.)
28. Only double Conn Smythe goalie
30. Hawk coach, Billy _____
33. 1969 Cup coach, Claude _____
34. Double Coach-of-the-Year
36. No. of Cups, Jean Beliveau
37. _____ the defense
38. 1st name, coach with most Cups
40. Player who _____ at home
42. Heavy _____
44. Win at all _____
47. 1987 Flyer playoff MVP, init.
48. Caps. goalie, init.
49. Detroit Soviet, init.
51. Ex-Hull playmaker, init.

CHAPTER

13

SUDDEN-DEATH OVERTIME

The very words conjure up an uneasy feeling, a dreadful sense of do or die. There's no second chance, no getting back the goal. Legends are created and championships lost in overtime. In this final quiz, we go into the extra period deadlocked. Anything can happen. Win or lose. Right or wrong. True or false. There are only two options.

(Answers are at the end of the chapter.)

13.1 It's only happened once: a Stanley Cup final in which every game ended in overtime. **T or F?**

13.2 Phil Esposito scored his first 50th-goal-in-a-season against his brother, Tony Esposito. **T or F?**

13.3 Jacques Plante made his rookie debut the same night Maurice Richard broke Nels Stewart's all-time scoring record in 1952. **T or F?**

13.4 In NHL history only six penalty shots have been awarded to players in the Stanley Cup finals. None have been successful. **T or F?**

13.5 Frozen pucks slide better on ice than pucks that aren't frozen. **T or F?**

13.6 Goalie Vladislav Tretiak, inducted in 1989, is the only Russian in the Hockey Hall of Fame. **T or F?**

13.7 Mario Lemieux scored his first NHL goal on his very first shot on net. **T or F?**

13.8 Gordie Howe is the only player whose number was retired in two NHL buildings. **T or F?**

13.9 Henri Richard has his name inscribed on the Stanley Cup more often than anyone else. **T or F?**

13.10 Peter Stastny was the first non–North American to win the NHL's Calder as Rookie of the Year. **T or F?**

13.11 Jacques Plante was the last goalie to win the Hart Trophy. **T or F?**

13.12 Only one goalie has ever won the Lady Byng Trophy for sportsmanship. **T or F?**

13.13 Eddie Shore was known as "The Human Express." **T or F?**

13.14 Since 1926, no playoff season has been completed without any overtime games. **T or F?**

13.15 Maurice and Henri Richard had a younger brother nicknamed "The Vest-Pocket Rocket." **T or F?**

13.16 Broadcaster Don Cherry played in only one NHL game. **T or F?**

13.17 Punch Imlach once coached Jean Beliveau. **T or F?**

13.18 NHLPA president Bob Goodenow was a back-up goalie for the Cleveland Barons in 1976–77. **T or F?**

13.19 Wayne Gretzky never graduated from high school. **T or F?**

13.20 Marcel Dionne never captained the L.A. Kings. **T or F?**

13.21 The new Montreal Forum will be built on the site of Expo 67. **T or F?**

SUDDEN-DEATH OVERTIME
Answers

13.1 True.

The Leafs–Canadiens rivalry has spawned many classic confrontations, the most exciting perhaps being the 1951 Cup finals, in which every game ended in overtime. While Rocket Richard scored in all five games, including once in overtime, Toronto clinched the Cup with overtime goals from Sid Smith, Ted Kennedy, Harry Watson and Bill Barilko.

13.2 False.

Phil scored his second 50th against brother Tony. His first got past the Kings' Denis DeJordy in 1971.

13.3 False.

The Rocket was supposed to pass Stewart's 324-goal milestone the night of Plante's first NHL game. Like the record-breaking point in 1989 that moved Gretzky past Howe's all-time scoring mark, the 1952 event generated great excitement. Twelve years had gone by since Stewart had retired, leaving few to challenge his record. Stewart was brought in for the opening ceremonies, and everyone waited for goal No. 325. Richard managed an assist but failed to score. Plante, not yet under contract, won his first NHL game but didn't witness Richard's historic moment, which came on November 8, 1952.

13.4 True.

Not once has a skater beaten a goalie on a penalty shot in Cup finals history. In recent times, Petr Klima failed against Rejean Lemelin in the 1990 Edmonton–Boston finals; Dave Poulin and Ron Sutter missed the mark against Grant Fuhr in consecutive games in the Edmonton–Philly finals in 1985; and Frank Mahovlich was stonewalled by Tony Esposito in the Montreal–Chicago finals in 1971.

13.5 True.

Whatever the physics are behind this phenomenon, it's a fact. That's why pucks are frozen solid for game use. Otherwise why would the NHL rule book call for it in Section 3, Rule 25, Paragraph B?

13.6 False.

Although he is the first and only Russian-trained *player* in the Hockey Hall of Fame, Tretiak is not the only Russian inductee, nor was he the first. That distinction belongs to famed coach Anatoli Tarasov, the father of Russian hockey. Tarasov was inducted in 1974.

13.7 True.

On October 11, 1984, in his first shift of his first NHL game, Lemieux scored his first NHL goal on his first shot on net.

13.8 False.

Two players have seen their jerseys retired by more than one team. The Whalers and the Red Wings retired Howe's No. 9, and another No. 9 received the same honour from the Jets and the Blackhawks: Bobby Hull.

13.9 False.

The Pocket Rocket has 11 Stanley Cups to his credit — but that record is only good enough for a tie with Toe

Blake, who has three Cups as a player and eight Cups as coach of the Canadiens.

13.10 False.

Czech-born Stastny won top rookie in 1981, making him not the first . . . or the second . . . but the third non–North American to win the Calder. In 1949, Pentti Lund of Finland was named Rookie of the Year, and Willi Plett from Paraguay took NHL rookie honours in 1977. (Lund was a Finnish-trained player; Plett learned in North America.)

13.11 True.

Not since Plante won the Hart in 1962 has a netminder been voted League MVP. There have been a number of runners-up (Fuhr, Liut and Vachon), but no winners. In fact, since 1924 only four goalies have received the award.

13.12 False.

The Lady Byng, honouring players who combine ability and sportsmanship, has never been awarded to a goalie.

13.13 False.

The Bruins' Eddie Shore was nicknamed "The Edmonton Express" (even though he was born in Saskatchewan). "The Human Express" was Charlie Conacher.

13.14 False.

The only year when all playoff games were decided in regulation time was 1963.

13.15 True.

To follow in the skate strides of "The Rocket" and "The Pocket Rocket" must have been difficult for brother Claude. Despite a try-out with the Canadiens, he's remembered only for his nickname: "The Vest-Pocket Rocket."

13.16 True.

Cherry's famous one-game career began and ended in Montreal during the 1955 Bruins–Canadiens playoffs. The NHL record books list no career goals, assists, penalties or fights for Grapes.

13.17 True.

Before turning pro with the Canadiens in 1953, Beliveau played for two years under Imlach, coach and GM of the Quebec Aces in the Quebec Senior League.

13.18 False.

The Players Association president has never played a game of professional hockey in his life.

13.19 True.

Gretzky is one credit shy of graduating. He had a business agent by the time most kids start high school, and before his classmates graduated he had signed his first professional hockey contract and was playing in the WHA.

13.20 True.

In 18 NHL seasons, Dionne only captained for one year, with the Red Wings in 1974–75.

13.21 False.

In 1995, the Montreal Canadiens will move into a new 22,000-seat arena built on the downtown site of Windsor Station. The historic railway station, to be integrated into the new hockey facilities, first became associated with the Canadiens when the team travelled to road games by rail.

SOLUTIONS TO GAMES

GAME 1: HOMETOWN BOYS

Part 1	Part 2
1. d	1. b
2. a	2. f
3. e	3. g
4. c	4. a
5. b	5. e
6. g	6. d
7. f	7. c

GAME 2: THE FIRST LINE

Left Wing	Centre	Right Wing
1. Lindsay	Abel	Howe
2. Martin	Perrault	Robert
3. Jackson	Primeau	Conacher
4. Krutov	Larionov	Makarov
5. Blake	Lach	Richard
6. Hatfield	Ratelle	Gilbert
7. Taylor	Dionne	Simmer
8. Shutt	Lemaire	Lafleur

GAME 3: THE HOCKEY BUILDERS

1. Lester Patrick
2. William Jennings
3. Conn Smythe
4. Jack Adams
5. Lord Stanley
6. Clarence Campbell
7. Art Ross
8. James Norris
9. Frank Calder
10. Dr. David Hart

GAME 4: ALL-STAR LINES

Part 1
1. Conn Smythe
2. Wall graffiti
3. Andre "The Moose" Dupont
4. Fred Shero
5. Jim Schoenfeld
6. Wayne Gretzky

Part 2
1. Don Cherry
2. Jacques Plante
3. Barclay Plager
4. Harry Neale
5. Gump Worsley
6. Bob Johnson

GAME 5: THE NAME OF THE GAME

Part 1	Part 2
1. g	1. f
2. i	2. i
3. e	3. b
4. m	4. m
5. a	5. c
6. k	6. a
7. j	7. k
8. d	8. e
9. f	9. g
10. c	10. j
11. h	11. l
12. b	12. h
13. l	13. d

GAME 6: ROOTS: FATHERS, SONS & BROTHERS

1. Ken & Dave Dryden
2. Lionel & Brian Conacher
3. Bobby & Brett Hull
4. Sam & Pete LoPresti
5. Brian & Terry Murray
6. Bryan Jr. & Ron Hextall
7. Barclay & Bob Plager
8. Gordie & Mark Howe
9. Phil & Tony Esposito
10. Bert & Ted Lindsay
11. Murray & Doug Wilson
12. Russ & Geoff Courtnall

GAME 7: THE WRITE STUFF

Part 1	Part 2
1. d	1. f
2. f	2. g
3. e	3. e
4. b	4. d
5. g	5. a
6. c	6. b
7. a	7. c

GAME 8: "HOW 'BOUT THEM TIGERS!"

Part 1	Part 2
1. c	1. c
2. f	2. e
3. e	3. b
4. a	4. d
5. d	5. a
6. b	6. g
	7. f

SOLUTIONS TO CROSSWORDS

CROSSWORD #1

CROSSWORD #2

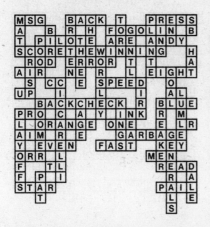

MSG Madison Square Garden
SB   Sean Burke
NE   New England
CC   Chris Chelios
LR   Luc Robitaille
TL   Trevor Linden

RN   Roger Neilson
MR   Maurice Richard
MO   Mark Osborne
TE   Tony Esposito
NJ   New Jersey
RW   Right Wing

CROSSWORD #3

CROSSWORD #4

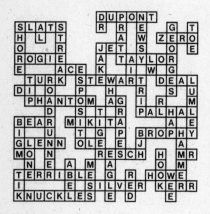

LW	Left Wing	
RL	Reggie Leach	
BJH	Bad Joe Hall	
DI	Dick Irvin	
AG	Adam Graves	

SR	Stephane Richer
OT	Overtime
DB	Daniel Berthiaume
SF	Sergei Fedorov
AO	Adam Oates
RH	Ron Hextall

ACKNOWLEDGEMENTS

The following publishers and organizations have given permission to use quoted material:

From *Net Worth: Exploding the Myths of Pro Hockey* by David Cruise and Alison Griffiths. Copyright © 1991 by David Cruise and Alison Griffiths. Reprinted by permission of Penguin Books Canada. From *The Hammer: Confessions of a Hockey Enforcer* by Dave Schultz with Stan Fischler. Copyright © 1981 by Dave Schultz and Stan Fischler. Published in Canada by Collins Publishers. Reprinted by permission of HarperCollins Canada. From *Gretzky: An Autobiography* by Wayne Gretzky with Rick Reilly. Copyright © 1990 by Wayne Gretzky. Reprinted by permission of HarperCollins Canada. From *The NHL 75th Anniversary Commemorative Book*. Copyright © 1991 by The NHL and Dan Diamond and Associates. Reprinted by permission of The NHL and Dan Diamond and Associates. From *The Last Season* by Roy McGregor. Copyright © 1983 by Roy McGregor. Published by Macmillan Canada. Reprinted by permission of Roy McGregor. From *Inside Maple Leaf Gardens* by William Houston. Copyright © 1989 by McGraw-Hill Ryerson. Reprinted by permission of McGraw-Hill Ryerson. From *The Game* by Ken Dryden. Copyright © 1983 by Ken Dryden. Reprinted by permission of Macmillan Canada. From *Hockey Hall of Fame* by Dan Diamond. Copyright © 1988 by Doubleday Canada. Reprinted by permission of Doubleday Canada. From *Conn Smythe: If You Can't Beat Them in the Alley* by Conn Smythe with Scott Young. Copyright © 1981 by Scott Young. Published by McClelland & Stewart. Reprinted by permission. From "Hockey Night in Canada," a CBC Sports Molstar Communications Presentation. Copyright © 1992 by The CBC. Reprinted by permission of The CBC.

Care has been taken to trace ownership of copyright material contained in this book. The publishers will take any information that will enable them to rectify any reference or credit in subsequent editions.